At the heart's farthest edge

Jan Fortune

Cinnamon Press
:: small miracles from distinctive voices ::

Published by Cinnamon Press,
Lytchett House
13 Freeland Park
Wareham Road
Poole
Dorset
BH16 6FA
www.cinnamonpress.com

Print Edition ISBN 978-1-78864-193-7
British Library Cataloguing in Publication Data. A CIP record for this book can be obtained from the British Library.

Cinnamon Press is represented by Inpress.

Designed and typeset in Adobe Garamond Pro by Cinnamon Press.
Cover design by Adam Craig © Adam Craig.
Illustrations by Adam Craig: hawthorn pp.3 & 178; oak and mistletoe pp.5, 9, 43, 65, 107, 145 & 180; dog rose pp.6 & 183; plantain p.10; sweet flag p.44; oxeye daisy p.66; angelica p.108, and elder p.146.

Note on herbs

The references to plants and herbal traditions in this book arise from experience, historical use, and cultural practice. They are offered in a spirit of reflection and relationship, not as diagnosis or medical advice. Readers with health concerns should consult a qualified practitioner.

For Dennie, with love and thanks.
And for Adam, always.

At the heart's farthest edge

Prologue

I wake in a foreign country, in a scrap of forest in the middle of nowhere, beside a love I've known only a decade. How did I get here?

Iona, June 1984. We have gathered for a week of retreat, to ponder our stories as women. We eat, cook, clean and sing together, walk the island, ending at Dun I, Iona's highest point, only three-hundred and thirty feet above sea level, but from here we can scan the whole of the island. North to the White Strand of the Monks. Martyr's Bay to the east. Columba's Bay to the south. The Bay at the Back of the Ocean to our west. On the way up we've stopped beside a rock pool, T*obar na h-Aoise*, the Well of Age. Washing in it is supposed to restore youth, but I'm twenty-three, believe I'll always be young. Still, I splash my face with the cool water.

Our guide reads the story of Elijah on Mount Carmel, running for his life after challenging the powers of his day. There is neither peace nor his god to be found as he encounters raging wind, earthquake and fire on the mountain. But a low whisper, a still small voice, calls him to leave his cave, his face covered by his cloak. And the question:

'What are you doing here, Elijah?'

Since moving from North Wales to Brittany in 2020, I've revisited moments so small, so slight, they might have vanished unnoticed. None of them were inevitable, but here I am in this forest, on a patch of earth that I am not indigenous to, yet feel is 'home'.

What are you doing here, Jan?

There are no final answers, only the next fork on the path and the flicker of light in the spaces between and beyond our ordinary, hurried perception. There are only more questions.

Behind me, along the branches of the path, are the people, creatures, things and expectations lost. But there are moments like this —

We set off from forest to coast, a long weekend in Plouhinec in the ground-floor of a tiny cabin owned by a welcoming young family who live upstairs and teach surfing in the season. It's November — no tourists or surfers, just a view across the bay and a box of comfort food to celebrate A.'s birthday. We've brought more books than we can read, warm woollens, rainproofs and walking boots. And a stack of notes for my imminent final herbal exam.

Each day we walk, write, read, cook, talk… and A. sits for me while I practise my diagnostic skills. He sits while I time his pulse, feel three pulse points at three levels on each wrist, listening for information about his energy, digestion, emotional and physical indicators, his heart… He sits with his tongue out, over and over, so I can make inferences about its coating, colour, shape, marks… talking him through the information he's heard before (so many times) as I touch, sense, attend…

There's an intimacy in these diagnostic tools, but A. is as aware as I am that I've long since learnt the information and techniques. Still, he sits while I go over and over them. Would anyone else agree to be 'examined' every day for a month, often twice, sometimes three times a day? On a birthday holiday?

This is a love letter to all the moments that, with no inevitability, brought me here.

My enchanted girl

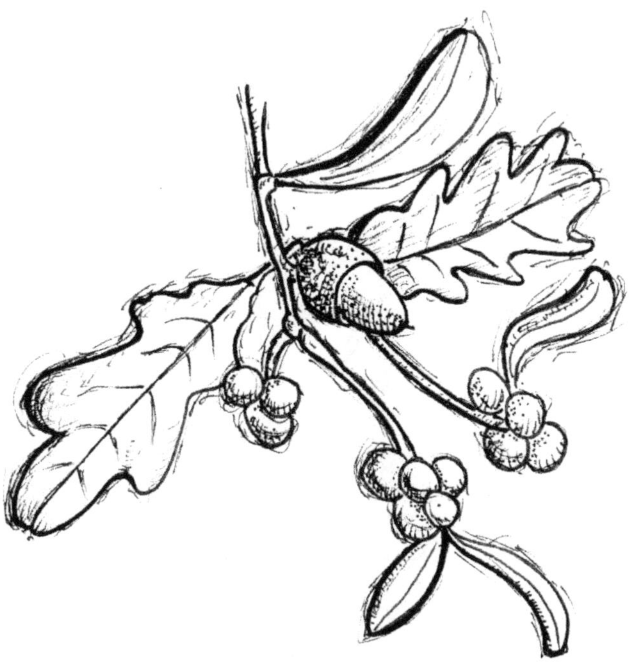

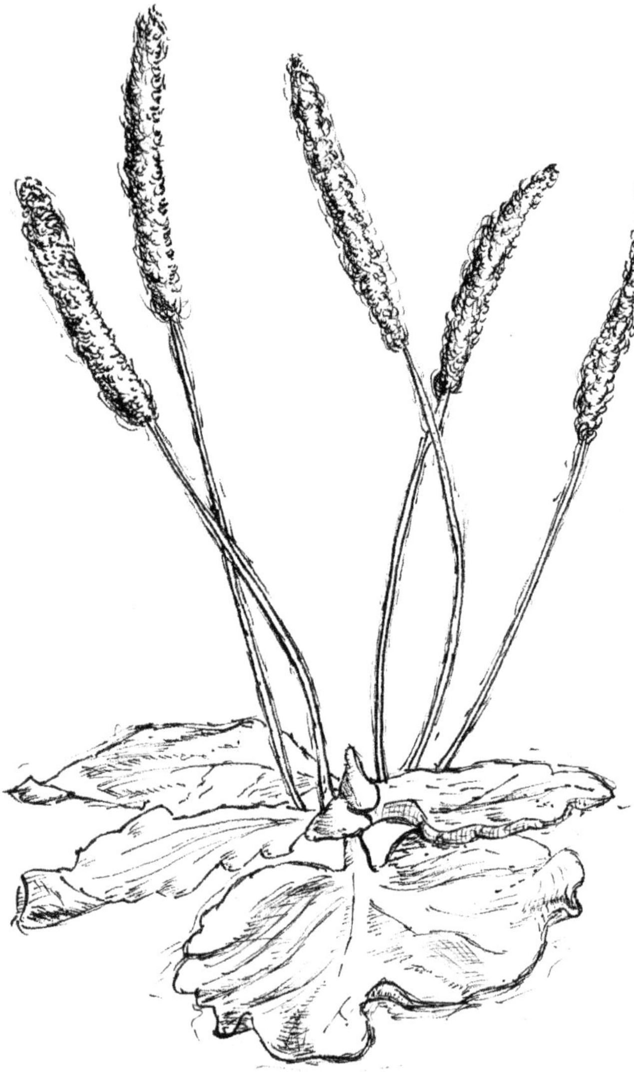

Being Casilda

Below us a panorama of river and concrete, sea and metal, L's house a brown dot, only fields away from the eighty square miles of cooling towers and flare stacks that litter the river, belching fire and smoke into a warm May day. I fix my gaze on the horizon where the blur of industry greys the land across the Tees, smudging into a sky of sulphur-tinged clouds that rise to a wash of salted blue.

Light splinters, haunting blues and sanguine reds puddle to gold.

A low hum.

Faces shimmer, beautiful and grotesque, strange familiars, familiar strangers. Warmth suffuses limbs no longer earthed, breeze stroking breath soft, softer…

and there is no time,

only a continuous moment

that swells to the sound of distant organ music,

dust motes shimmying in pools

of red and blue falling on stone.

A hand on my arm. I blink, the view returning — panorama of river and concrete, sea and metal…

Away with the faeries, I say, shaking myself back to the world. I take the plastic thermos of lemonade L is holding out to me.

She nods, stretches, lays back on the springy ground, soaking up the heat of the day.

We've skirted along Kettle Beck through ash and oak trees shading bluebells, their scent thick with dreaming, stepped over cinder-black slugs, ascended a bank littered with the iron workings that drew my ancestors here, leaving behind hunger in Ireland or the even harsher conditions of slate mines in Wales. Higher up are more metal workings, long gone — a Bronze Age settlement excavated of its axe heads and secrets, imagined now from the shape of the steep bank where heather will purple in autumn. It has taken us two hours to reach the fort. Draco's Rock, L calls it. On the pinnacle of the nab, an obelisk of sandstone bricks, once a lookout tower and beacon to warn of invasion during the Napoleonic Wars. Later, a house, demolished and rebuilt as a landmark to the ironstone mining in the hills.

Silly Silda, L says, leaning on an elbow and pouring cool lemonade made by her mother. You're not really of this world. You weren't a thousand years ago.

I smile, lie down next to her in the grass. And are you?

Ah, now there's the rub, she says, and closes her eyes.

It started like this —

We are arrayed in rows, desks joined in pairs, twenty-eight eleven-year-old girls in stiff navy-blue pinafores. The girl I share a desk with in this alphabetical arrangement is called Susan and has spread her pencils across the desk. I nudge them back towards her side. At the front of the class another girl, not much taller than me, chats with the teacher as though they are old friends. Fine strawberry-blonde hair, an easy laugh. Mrs G tells her to choose someone to assist her as the class book-monitor.

She points to me.

I chose you for your plaits, she tells me on the way to the stationery office. If you get out of hand I can pull on them.

I scowl.

She laughs. But really I recognised you — always so small and pale. We've been so many people, some famous, some no-one's heard of. We were most ourselves as Ben Haddaj and Casilda. I always recognise you.

She smiles at my puzzlement. You'll soon understand.

Over lunch, she asks what my favourite flower is.

Rose, I say. Oh and hawthorn. I love daisies too. They…

Tell me about roses.

I love them all. Dog roses in Kirkleatham. They look fragile but have big red thorns. Faeries use the hips to make themselves invisible.

Faeries?

I nod, return to the roses — My dad grows cultivated ones with beautiful names. They're delicate, fussy about their soil, you have to protect them from greenfly. A lot of work, but special…

Antoine de Saint-Exupéry, L interrupts.

Who?

He wrote *The Little Prince.* I see you'll need a reading list.

> It's the time you have wasted for your rose that makes your rose so important… You become responsible forever for what you've tamed.

She grins. Perhaps you'll tame me.

At the end of the day Mrs G asks to talk to me. She'd chosen L as the book-monitor so that she would have the chance to talk to the other girls about L while she was out of the room. L is 'different' — diabetic, we must watch out for odd signs that might mean she's becoming ill. If she seems dizzy or a little manic…

She seems to like you, she says. Take good care of her.

I nod, remember bringing a tea towel for my parents to dry their eyes when they argued, two- or three-years-old. Yes, I'll take care of her.

While we wait for the bus to pull into the school car-park that evening, L tells me the story of Casilda and the roses, how she would take bread to the prisoners in the dungeons of the Alcázar in Moorish Toledo. One evening her father discovered her on the stairs down to the cells and asked what she was carrying in her dress. Roses, Casilda said, fainting. And, as her father caught her, roses, not bread, fell from the folds.

A shadow pale as dust flits across a mote of light, the fragrance of roses suffusing the air. Somewhere a string is plucked, faint music —

Al-'ūdu qud tarannam

Bi-abdā'i talhīn

Wa ŝaqqod al-mad ā nib

Riyād al-basātîn

...a sound of water against stone. Is there a word in the breeze? Tulaytula.

...a rustle of silk, shadows beneath vaulted arches... water bells against stone, whispers, Casilda.

Jan! L's hand is on my arm, shaking me. I blink. No-one has ever shortened my name to Jan before.

The bus is here, L says. You were miles away.

Sorry, I was... Can you smell roses?

Throughout secondary school, I attended elocution lessons, studying speech and drama with a young woman in love with a local pop star. Billy did not return her affection. The lessons began when a friend's mother begged me to accompany her daughter so that FC would learn to speak properly and 'get on in life'. FC quickly dropped out, but I persisted into sixth form, performed dramatic readings at Eisteddfods, joined a local amateur dramatics company and eventually made a choice between drama school and university. I learnt poetry and a love of language sitting on a bench in an almost empty room, my plump, disappointed-in-love, young teacher behind a desk in the bow window. But I learnt performance from L as we role-played our way through seven years. We became a cast of personae, amongst them a race of immortals and souls of the people we had been across time. But we were, above all, Casilda and Ben Haddaj.

Despite, or perhaps because of L's mother's efforts to separate us, we cleaved to each other. And with L, I attended concerts and operas, listened to her playing Chopin preludes, discovered literature that I would have found nowhere else, watched the TV version of Robert Graves's *I, Claudius* with her parents (banned in my house, perhaps because my mother had grown up with enough inter-familial warring and violence), and ate food that had texture and flavour. At home food came from packets or tins, cheap cuts of meat on Sundays, roasted to destruction to guard against 'germs'.

At weekends L and I hiked in the hills above her house, her mother rolling her eyes as we set out — me in white — being Casilda.

Once there was a Moorish princess, Casilda, daughter of the king of Toledo and a Berber girl who died in childbirth. Casilda had long golden hair, green eyes, pale skin. She wore only white or the palest blue, almost white, like the halo of sky around the sun.

In the autumn, the fields below Eston hills filled with bramble pickers, but in summer the fruits were small and green, the thorns vicious. We'd negotiate the steeply rising track, crowded on either side by tall ferns and alders, fat bluebottles buzzing around us.

We'll make for Draco's Rock, L would say, climb to the top.

Casilda's warring father, Alamun, was the last Moorish ruler of Toledo. He'd filled his dungeons with Christian knights, captured in battle by his son, Ahmed. Casilda was unlike her family, especially her half-sister, Zoraida, fiery, dark and obsessed with reading romances. Ahmed decided that Zoraida should marry Ben Haddaj, a prince of Zaragoza. He was everything Zoraida wanted, but he didn't love Zoraida. And perhaps he wasn't even a prince…

At night Ben Haddaj would hide in the shadows to glimpse Casilda taking food to the prisoners. In the dungeons she learnt their stories and gave her heart to a different god. Knowing that he could never be with Casilda, Ben Haddaj returned to the Jewish faith of his ancestors and died making his way to the Holy Land, but not before he'd healed Casilda of a debilitating illness so that she was able to travel to Burgos to begin her life as a saint.

L would repeat the story as we made our way, panting, uphill.

But we live on, she repeated, born generation after generation until we are re-united.

My plaits were brown, not golden, my eyes brown, rimmed in black. These were signs of enchantment, L insisted. And I would see Ben Haddaj before me. The story and the facts became one. Belief was my gift.

May 2018, just after my fifty-seventh birthday. I've come to Zaragoza with A. to research a novel that includes the elusive Ben Haddaj. It's a labyrinthine place where I get lost on every trip to the market, certain that the streets move overnight. The city buzzes with treasures — an amphitheatre of the former Roman city of Cesaraugusta and the Aljafería Palace, Ben Haddaj's home.

We visit on a blistering day, sit under trellised arches listening to water tinkle along irrigation channels into a pool, finches celebrating their nests in the plump orange trees, fruit hanging like Christmas tree ornaments. We marvel at the Great Hall and courtyard and I leave A. photographing exquisite white arches while I cross the north portico and stand in the doorway of the tiny oratory, where once Ben Haddaj worshipped.

Alone in the tiny mosque's cool dark shadows, I imagine Ben Haddaj making his last prayers as a Muslim before boarding a ship to Jerusalem, a place he would never reach.

There is no clear record of Caliph Ismael Ben Haddaj. Was he a prince or a vizier or perhaps nephew to Vizier Hasdai of Córdoba? Was he an alchemist or a myth? And what has he to do with me?

What are you doing here?

The guidebook tells me that the intertwined arches would once have been covered in plasterwork ornamented with plant motifs. The horseshoe archway over the mihrab on the qibla wall, pointing the way to the Kaaba in Mecca, is a small copy of the one in the Mezquita of Córdoba. The square resembles an octagon, though it's a square with the corners chamfered off and the room rises towards a gallery of small-lobed archways inscribed with the Kufic characters of Surahs. The plant and geometric designs, the intricate latticework, dapple in the light. I look towards the domed ceiling and back to the niche where…

Ben Haddaj stands, hands raised as though in surrender, his back to me, facing the mihrab. The hood and fabric of his burnous are thrown back. His qamis, which falls to his knees, is of the same cotton as his sirwal and he doesn't wear a turban, but a simple taqiyah, similar to a Jewish yarmulke.

Allahu Akbar, he says, as he places his right hand over his left and begins to recite the Istiftah Du'aa, his voice clear but soft.

subhanakal-lahumma

wabihamdika watabarakas-muka wata'aala

judduka wala ilaha ghayruk.

a'auodu billaahi minash-shaytaanir rajeem

bis-millaahir rahmaanir raheem

Words I have not heard before. After them the Surah Al-Fatiha:

Bismillaahir Rahmaanir Raheem

Alhamdu lillaahi Rabbil 'aalameen

Allahu Akbar, as he bends and intones three times, *Subhanna Rabbiyal Adheem.*

He stands, raises his arms, still reciting, prostrates himself, palms to the floor, repeating three times, *Subhanna Rabbiyal A'laa.* Rises to his knees, hands on the floor. Even more softly he whispers, *llaahumma-ghfir lee warhamnee wajburnee, warfa'nee, wa 'aafinee war'zuqnee.*

O Allah, forgive me, have mercy on me, strengthen me, raise me in status, pardon me and grant me provision.

Allahu Akbar. He stands and begins again, going through the rak'ah three more times. Finally, his voice so low I can scarcely hear:

O Allah, forgive me, have mercy on me, strengthen me, raise me in status, pardon me and grant me provision... Hear, O Israel! The Lord is our God, the Lord is one! You shall love the Lord your God with all your heart and with all your soul and with all your might...

He turns, smiles in my direction. And I shiver in the heat as he lifts a hand in salute and...

Ah, there you are, A. says behind me.

Often, as we walked in the hills, L would pull me to crouching. An elderly couple might pass, a fat beagle panting behind them. Or a family group.

Scouts, she'd tell me, sent to re-capture Casilda after she left Toledo to be baptised.

Ahmed won't rest till he returns you to Toledo. There are spies everywhere. And he hates me for rejecting Zoraida. If he finds us, there's no saying what he'd be capable of.

L would stand, peering at the back of a retreating couple and their dog.

He's hunting with hounds, but we're safe for the moment. Move quickly. Keep to the side of the track.

At Draco's Rock we'd spread cardigans on the dusty ground, sit to share L's mother's picnic — moist chicken, homemade raspberry jam on homemade bread. The lemonade cold in the flask, grains of flesh floating in tart liquid.

I learnt the directions of the wind, the times of sunset, that enchantment could be shared.

Together we inhabited the terrain of an animate world we nestled into —

sphagnum

yarrow

sneezewort

angelica

ling

harebell

hawthorn

thistle

rosebay willowherb

groundsel

gorse

cow parsley

bramble

purple moor grass

daisy

broom

eyebright

dandelion

coltsfoot

red campion

elder

Somewhere a string is plucked, faint music —

the scent of roses…

Ben Haddaj

Cleveland Grammar was run by two fiercely intelligent women, ambitious for every girl in their care. A visitor walking in might have thought the place ran on military discipline, but the only 'rules' I remember were 'walk on the left', 'don't bring oranges to school' (the headteacher, LC, had migraines triggered by citrus) and 'if you don't want to learn, don't spoil it for others'. Male teachers were rare. It took me into my forties to realise there had been several couples amongst the women teachers. Not all of them were 'qualified', but if LC recognised talent that was what counted. I remember little bullying and when, on one occasion, two girls physically fought one another, one of the girls returned from her visit to LC's office bemused. There was no detention, no recrimination, but JT had learnt more than she wanted to know about the principles of peace, in particular how astronauts were trained to be able to tolerate one another in intense conditions, how vital this skill would be for her one day.

It was a forgiving place, but L's uninhibited honesty, together with what appeared to adolescents in '70s Teesside to be 'strange' interests, marked her as 'different'.

Can she really do it?

What? I ask the gathering group of girls.

Can she really get in touch with dead people? All that, what does she call it? Free writing?

You should ask her yourself, I reply.

I did. She told me she doesn't talk to *hoi polloi*. I just wanted to contact my gran.

Are you sure? I mean it might be… upsetting…

Maybe, she concedes, then goes on, but that free writing thing is weird. It got me thinking…

It's called automatic writing. Psychography.

Yeah? I saw her doing it yesterday. She looked completely out of it. She told CT she goes to other places… when she's in that… whatever it is… and that she 'gets' these other people…

Talking behind my back, I see. L glowers at the group of girls.

Well, show us then, W goads. If you can get these other people from wherever, dead or outer space…

L's eyes narrow.

Ignore them, I whisper.

Aw, come on. Let her show us.

We just want to see, G says mildly, smiling at both of us. We're interested. Is it like a trance? I mean, do people really take over your body? Dead people?

It's more complicated, L says.

I shake my head, mouth 'no'. Tell them you've got a headache, tell them you feel a hypo coming on, I say in my head.

I get people from the past. Some of them are myself, past lives. I'm not like you.

Someone makes a farting noise with her mouth.

Psychography is metaphysical, it's… L begins.

Come again in English, W retorts. Laughter like gulls squawking. W circles her index finger around the side of her head, the sign for 'lunatic'.

L sighs theatrically, closes blue-grey eyes slowly, moves her head, her newly-cut bell of strawberry-blonde hair shimmering. Give me a piece of paper. Large. And a sharp pencil, not too sharp, so it doesn't break while I'm in flow.

Tools are produced. L sits at a desk, *Sally4Macco* scored into an inked heart at its centre, the throng of girls moving closer.

Not too close, L warns. I need absolute silence. Anyone who doesn't believe should leave now. I'll be in a delicate state, the slightest negative influence could have consequences.

Several girls glance at W.

Don't look at me. I'll believe if I see it for myself.

I think she should leave, L says.

No way.

I think you should, G says, and other girls murmur assent.

She's bonkers, W spits back, flouncing from the room, heavy door slamming the silence.

Half an hour later I deliver L to the nurse's room. She's ice-pale and shaky, vision blurring, blood sugar falling, commanding me to stop fussing as she sways unsteadily, triumphant and unrepentant, having convinced more of the class that she is not as other mortals.

If a lion could speak, we wouldn't understand him, L says grimly as she slumps onto the bed in the nurse's room.

L was my bridge to a world of intellect and culture. What did I bridge for her?

I was used to negotiating volatile environments in a rowdy extended family — my mother's eight surviving siblings, thirty cousins and counting. Used to gauging emotions, knowing when to become invisible. But my introversion belied a steely confidence, 'stubbornness' was a word I heard often.

I won peer approval by speaking truth to power. When our English teacher, feared and formidable, decided we would read *Lorna Doone* after finishing *Silas Marner,* the girls got together to ask me to intercede. I did, pointing out that having just made their way through George Eliot's story of the Weaver of Raveloe, a book L and I saw as a banquet, but left most reeling with indigestion, they needed a break, were in no state to tackle Blackmore's 'phonological' style of seventeenth century Exmoor dialect.

Twenty-eight thirteen- and fourteen-year-olds held a single breath as I spoke. Mrs D nodded agreement. Later that year she was less impressed when I refused to leave the room so that she could talk L out of taking Latin as one of her O-level options. L did not want to be dissuaded and I insisted on staying to advocate (with all the determination of my socialist trade-unionist grandfather). Mrs D hissed that I could be so self-righteous, and then, as though she'd shocked herself, that she wished she had my tenacity.

Nairn, 1976. Against L's mother's better judgement, I'd been taken on their family holiday.

I'm huddled with L in the tiny bedroom of a caravan on Nairn beach after a long walk on a sweltering July morning, along white sand that crunched and sang beneath our feet.

The police had left and L was finally asleep, her breath catching as she turned. Did she whisper something? I stroked her face, still wet, leant forward, brushed lips against salt dew, too soft to be a kiss, but her eyes opened and she held out her arms.

I see her on the beach, hurling a stone at the naked man who had me imprisoned in a sticky grasp, hissing, Everything will be all right as long as you don't struggle. Just take your clothes off, everything will be alright. Hands around my throat, rough breath, white cotton tearing…

The stone hitting.

Our feet on white sand, rub of grains keening above the percussion of waves, both of us running hard before L's sudden halt, winded, the man catching up, grabbing her, the noise that came from her. And me, turning, shouting as I ran back, sand squealing under my feet. When did I lift the rock? The story and the facts must match, keep track, you must keep track or it's the end of the story.

Running again.

How long? How far?

We scaled a fence into a pine plantation and I gave L my shoes. She had lost a sandal as we ran and couldn't limp barefoot through pine needles and stones. Her diabetic feet would be prone to infection. We walked and walked, stumbled on a picnicking family with two young children, broke down, weeping, garbling the story of a man on the beach…

I'm your Ben Haddaj, L told me through tears. I'm supposed to save you, my enchanted girl.

I nodded. I was not Janet Fortune from the Riverdale Estate.

Once, Ben Haddaj had opened the way for Casilda's new life. What had she offered him in return?

Perhaps the permission to choose his path?

In this lifetime would Ben Haddaj save me as he had yearned to do a thousand years ago or would I…?

Cephas

A thousand years ago in Moorish Toledo, Ben Haddaj's love for Casilda went unrequited. Casilda, pale, suffering from an ailment that made her continually bleed, often faint and fatigued, left Toledo to be baptised in Burgos. From there she went to live beside a healing well in the wooded mountains close to Briviesca.

Now her cave is dwarfed by a lavish sanctuary and church, a gold vault adorned with a sculpture of Casilda in repose, her dress rich red and gold. Some legends say she lived as a healer till she was over a hundred years old, others that she died young. All say she lived as a hermit, befriended by local villagers and mountain lions. Whatever her fragility, she had a vision for her life that Ben Haddaj could not shake.

He wanted to save her.

She wanted her own path.

Belief might be my gift, but I was less than biddable.

On two occasions L instructed me not to go on school trips. The logistics of keeping insulin cold and managing her diet did not allow L such travel, but she assured me she would never think of going on such awful journeys — forced marches around tourist spots, hearing tired scripts from underpaid guides. Days marred by noisy social events, no doubt compulsory. Girls trying to find local boys to humiliate themselves with. I would hate it and shouldn't go.

She was not wrong, but I could disappear into my own world whenever overwhelm threatened and I yearned to see beyond Teesside — a woodland retreat in Austria with a trip to Salzburg, a ski-ing trip in central France. On both, I could vanish into my cocoon, but was awed by the architecture of Salzburg, the forest where we got up before dawn and hiked through snow, landscape uneven and startling, owls calling the sun to rise — long-eared owls with their low *hoos*, tawny owls with their rapid *kewicks*, the shrill of barn owls and plosive *kweeos* of little owls.

I soaked in their calls, unaware of my school shoes letting in snow, my coat unequal to the pre-dawn cold. Vision blurred, no scent of ice or taste of wind, only voices thrumming through heart and throat.

As the fancy dress party to be held at the end of the week approached, my English teacher gently told me not to worry — I could go as myself if I didn't want to dress up. Instead, I raided the centre's box of fabrics and materials, kept for this event, and appeared as Athena. My robe a scratchy length of thick curtain fabric patterned with gold leaves, tied with string at the waist. I carried a plaster owl, an ornament with a chipped ear found on a windowsill above the stairs. It was judged the evening's best outfit even though I sat in a corner of the room, watching others dance while I cradled the crumbling owl, thinking of calls in the forest to drown out the music.

In France, skiing was cut short when my geography teacher lost control on the slope and hurtled into me. My right knee ballooned, ached and popped. I was given painkillers and a thick elastic bandage and hobbled each day from the bus to the little glass café to watch the others, my injured leg on a chair, reading or drifting into worlds of my own. I carried with me an owl-head pebble, carved from alabaster and with round yellow eyes. My owl had no ear-tufts—*chouette*, not *hibou*. I'd found her on the day before the accident in a local shop full of tourist trinkets and I have her still, a tiny talisman. In France I slept through dawns, but each night I stayed awake to hear the owls in the snow-dense forest beneath the slopes.

short-eared owl

long-eared owl

scops owl

tawny owl

little owl

eagle owl

barn owl

tengmalm's owl

pygmy owl

Despite my forays, by the end of O-levels the suspension of disbelief we inhabited remained intact. After our exams, we hiked the Lake District, stayed in youth hostels and read poetry out loud from mountainsides above grey-blue tarns and, one day, got a lift from a coach-load of American women tourists concerned for two children hiking alone. Neither of us looked sixteen.

For the rest of the summer I was on a mission. Our church had hosted a weekend conference on the subject of 'vocation', with visits from a Franciscan Brother and a Church Army Captain and Sister. And I'd been recruited to join the Church Army Captain on a beach mission in Bridlington.

I had no experience of evangelical Christianity, but was promised a summer away from home helping with children's activities by the sea. We were billeted with local families and four of us, the girls in a group of twelve recruits, were housed in a tiny caravan owned by a local church family. It was parked in a large, wild garden that filled with bats each evening. I was the only one enchanted.

By day we used a modern church building as our base, full of puppets and art supplies, with a little kitchen where we cooked inadequate meals, though I hardly ate through my teens, unless I was at L's house. The worship space was a cold, white box that didn't look or feel like church, but it did have one beautiful window, a long rectangle of abstract stained glass. I could stand in front of it and fall into another world, one I'd been visiting since I was four years old, a world where I'd become Casilda, where plants and owls whispered to me, and all that existed were pools of light on a floor, music that I couldn't name and a dance of faces that watched me across time.

And then I discovered Cephas. Along the coast, in Saltburn, was a church youth group that our new parish priest encouraged me to join. At its height, Cephas numbered a hundred or more young people who crowded into a community hall every Sunday evening. On the evening I turned up, I was greeted by a young man in his mid-twenties. D had dropped out of a philosophy degree at Warwick University after taking part in the student rent strike and a month-long occupation of the Senate House in spring 1975. Unusually, I was wearing dungarees over my white blouse, on which I'd embroidered JOY across the bib. D nodded, grinned, said, I like people who wear their names on their breasts.

It's not my name, I corrected him, it's our Sunday School motto —Jesus, Others, Yourself — JOY.

He considered a moment. Interesting. How's that going for you?

D was an anarchist. After the summer, he and his girlfriend, Y, moved into the attic of a house owned by another Cephas member, together with a fourth house-mate and 'The House' became Cephas's home in its swan song days.

That first night, around forty people aged eighteen to twenty-eight gathered. I was the baby, just turned sixteen. The evening's theme was an extempore performance of Brecht's *The Caucasian Chalk Circle,* followed by a discussion of justice, power, class struggle, religious hypocrisy… Later they broke for drinks before singing choruses — not the kind I would later encounter in an evangelical theological college — The Incredible String Band's 'You Get Brighter' featured most weeks, along with Dylan songs and Taizé chants in Latin.

The person I married at the age of eighteen was a stalwart of Cephas. The person L married a few years later was the cousin of the boyfriend of a girl who'd been a member for years. When the group became too small to go on hiring the community hall, due to an exodus leaving for university that year, we moved to The House and became an intense band of a dozen regulars with a handful of others who sporadically returned to share stories of the glory days.

Once, there had been whole coaches setting off for summers in the community of Taizé near Cluny in Burgundy. The community had been started by the Swiss Protestant, Roger Schütz, in a farmhouse during the Second World War, taking in refugees from occupied France. Gradually other brothers joined what became an ecumenical community. It appealed to youth across the world, pilgrims who flocked to share discussions inspired by the rising tide of liberation theology. D and Y didn't believe in state weddings, but had been 'married' by Brother Roger in Taizé.

At The House, we went on singing Taizé's Latin chants, songs by Dylan, Steely Dan, The Incredible String Band… We spent weekends playing Dungeons and Dragons, amiably arguing about gender politics, class, anarchist theory and the merits of Kate Bush. The music, a world away from the classical music and opera L had introduced me to, was a revelation. And the politics fascinating, reminding me of my dad's arguments with his socialist father.

I'm standing at the bus stop in Saltburn after a Sunday evening of Cephas. I huddle under a white knitted tam o' shanter and a blanket in shades of blue, one of my nanna's box of cast-offs, which I've cut and sewn into the shape of a cloak. L is not with me, perhaps she's not well or visiting a sister. The boy beside me is in his early twenties, shaggy curly hair the shade of wet sand and a broad grin.

I usually have a car but it broke down.

I nod. Everyone knows the tragic story of the love of M's life. She'd moved to Sheffield and he visited every weekend till she told him that she was seeing the son of a local scrap-metal merchant and, though it was early days, the sex was promising. His trusty Mini had given up its life on the return journey from their last weekend together.

I invited you to my birthday party, he says. You didn't come.

I didn't think you meant it.

He looks quizzical.

I thought you just invited everyone in the room so you wouldn't feel awkward about leaving anyone out.

He nods. You probably wouldn't have enjoyed it. Lot of drink. You're what? Fourteen?

Sixteen. Seventeen in May.

Yeah? He brightens, grins. I like your hat.

It's another four months before he asks me out, just after the end of year exams, halfway through my two years of A-levels.

We'll meet at Pacitto's, he says.

I wait by the ice-cream parlour for almost an hour, eventually walk down the strand to the cabin Pacitto's only open during the summer holidays. He's not there. I meet him as I walk back. He was about to give up, he says. He meant the ice-cream parlour at the Marske end of the beach, nearer where he lives. The one I didn't know existed.

We don't get ice-cream.

We sit on the tussocky grass at Coatham looking over South Gare where fisherman's huts jostle with the lumbering towers of steel industry on reclaimed land around the breakwater of the Tees, wind whipping up sand despite the early June sun. When he kisses me, I sink within myself.

Somewhere a horse chestnut has just been struck by lightning, half of it split away and I recite the names of the captive moths I feel, beating their wings around my heart —

flame carpet

brimstone

clouded border

peppered moth

buff-tip

antler moth

silver ground carpet

latticed heath

chimney sweeper

gold swift

In the summer after taking A-levels, I began to wear more colours, using my eighteenth birthday money to buy a long Indian hippie dress in purples.

On this day I'm wearing a cheesecloth shirt with a square, embroidered yoke, a tiered, pink floral skirt over a broderie anglaise petticoat. My straw hat matches my long-handled woven basket and I bundle a crocheted shawl into it as we set off.

The House is decamping to the beach on a hot June day. Summer and Cambridge are ahead. My mother hasn't yet issued her ultimatum, though things are tense and I often stay over in Saltburn rather than returning home to see if the mood is rage or tears.

We carry Tupperware boxes of sandwiches and a big sponge cake down to the shore. AT sets us off singing 'Alice's Restaurant', M joining in with guitar, a shiny spruce Ovation with mother of pearl inlay on the fingerboard and its Lyrachord plastic back. An instrument that AT, a better guitarist, covets. M tells me Lyrachord was developed by NASA for its acoustic properties as well as being lightweight. I'm in my sixties before I discover it had nothing to do with NASA.

Belief is my gift. One day my children will laugh, call it gullibility. But today —

marram grass

gorse

sea kale

thrift

kelp

sea holly

bindweed

aster

kidney vetch

broom

Later, headachy from sun and not enough water, Y tells me to nap in the attic she shares with D. It smells of patchouli joss sticks and bright shawls cover the chairs and lamps. When I wake it's cool and I pull my crocheted shawl from the basket and throw it over the cheesecloth shirt. Pulling apart my unkempt plait, I comb fingers through hair that falls below my waist before making my way down the narrow stairs to drink water from the tap in the bathroom and splash my face.

I wonder if M will still be at The House or have gone back to the place he's recently begun to rent with his friend, IS. In the hallway, D looks up as I descend the stairs.

About to start a game of D&D, he says. It'll probably go on late but you can stay the night if you like. He pauses. And M, if you like. There's another pause. Are you two… I mean… He trails off. You'll be fine once you get to Cambridge, he adds.

Somewhere in the years of sixth form and Cephas, the bubble that enveloped me and L — strange, intense — stretched thin.

We had loved one another for centuries.

And then…

Does the moth ache for the cocoon?

In 2014 the Mariinsky Opera staged the whole of Wagner's *Ring Cycle* in Birmingham. It had only been staged in the UK twice before. L had passed on the love of this music and I went with my oldest child, R — four long evenings of extraordinary drama and music.

On the second night I noticed a woman who looked like the woman L might have become, approached her to ask if she was indeed L. She wasn't. I found it hard to imagine L would not be there.

But listening to the music, we were together, somewhere we always are…

Marry or burn

The young vicar of St Cuthbert's Kirkleatham, IF, had grown up locally. Returning, he proved that a prophet was not welcome in his own country. To many, he remained an 'upstart boy', his Cambridge theology degree pretentious, though not to LC and her deputy PR, a mathematician who wore tweed skirts and twin sets and drove a fast sports car to church.

IF adopted me as an ally and intellectual collaborator. His two-year confirmation course bored the ears off the group of eleven- and twelve-year-olds who attended every Saturday morning. All but me. When I was twelve, he began loaning me theology books so we could discuss them. A couple of years later he started taking me to Deanery Synod meetings to learn the workings of church politics. One meeting stood out because he told me that the subject that evening was my future. A debate on women's ordination. Considering that women were not allowed to so much as clean the sanctuary beyond the altar rail at St Cuthbert's, the young priest's move was a bold one. A prophet despite his own home.

I remember nothing of the debate except that is was acrimonious. Did IF's words — 'it's about your future' — start a chain of thought that led to me being priested at the first service of the ordination of women in the Church of England?

IF left a few years later and the new minister, CL, was more evangelical. When I was in sixth form he carried on a heated debate with my radical A-level Religious Studies teacher, JS, who had left the too-narrow-confines of Methodist ministry. I was their go-between. IF had encouraged me to doubt, question and wonder. JS delighted in my willingness to parry theological questions, while CL warned me theology would rot my faith. I went ahead and applied to IF's Cambridge college to study theology, having discovered that

Cambridge was apparently so old and well-respected that I would have to take extra entrance exams.

The change of vicar had no impact on the other dominant person of church life. MJS was my Sunday School teacher from the age of seven. She'd fought a battle with IF to insist that girls should wear veils at their Confirmation service (and lost). She'd trained me as one of her Sunday School assistants from the age of twelve and provided a safe haven from my home. But her conservatism ran deep. At the end of June, my mother's ultimatum to stop seeing M or get out of the house was delivered, and I left to live with M. MJS called us in for an interview and insisted we must marry. Between my mother's threats and MJS's terrifying belief that my soul was in eternal danger, I organised the wedding in haste.

Marrying quickly appealed to M. He had failed to dissuade me from going to Selwyn and worried that I would leave him behind if I went to university alone. When I'd insisted on taking the Cambridge entrance exams, he'd proposed in the lounge of The Zetland Hotel, Saltburn.

What would you say *if* I asked you to marry me? was barely audible over the sound of a raucous band called The Crabs, which, for many years, I believed was a reference to crustaceans.

If you asked I'd say yes, fell out of me before I'd engaged either gut or brain, and was immediately accepted.

I married M three weeks before going to Cambridge, the wedding so speedily arranged that people were startled to discover I wasn't pregnant. The Lay Reader from St Cuthbert's walked me down the aisle in the absence of family. A school-friend, E, and another from Cephas, K, were bridesmaids, in home-made dresses of stretchy blue nylon.

L was to be my maid of honour, but stopped answering the phone when I called. A few days before the wedding, a parcel appeared outside the door of the bungalow I shared with M and IS, his best friend from school days. It contained tiny pastry forks and a note from L — she could not support this marriage and would be going to stay with her sister in the Lake District for a few weeks.

I have no idea what became of the pastry forks, but L's honesty and instinct I carry still.

I married M on September 22, 1979. I can't visualise the flowers the church was decorated with, but I remember that my headteacher and English teacher, LC, had bought and arranged them.

In the stippled light beneath oak leaves, as we stood stiffly for photos after the service, M leant across me to shake hands with his best man, IS, the two of them laughing as though they had sealed a bargain. During the service the vicar omitted one word. A tiny slip? There was no vow to 'obey', but words of power had been spoken and would take three decades to unravel.

What brought me to Finistère on the cusp of turning sixty?

Brexit played a part in wanting to leave the UK, though we'd been toying with the idea of a move for a couple of years.

A succession of moments, thresholds cradling the next and the next. My first day at senior school when L chose me across centuries or a row of desks. A young curate who told my future. The day I walked into Cephas and met M. They could have led to so many places, but here I am in the forest.

From inside St Cuthbert's, soaring notes of Bach swim into the bright autumn day. The world tilts and there is only light. Shimmering cobalt and carmine, pooling on gold leaves strewn on green grass.

Samhain to Imbolc

October 31, 2023…

Dusk falls, softening Samhain light. I could reach out and cup it in my hands. Autumn is turning to winter, days folding in on themselves. In the face of the horror exploding in Palestine, it's impossible not to be keenly aware of mortality. This year Samhain feels like the shadow answer to the poet Mary Oliver when she asks, in the poem 'The Summer Day', what we will make of our wild and precious life, the only one we have.

When we moved here three years ago, the living room wall ran with water, not damp but a cascade that wasn't apparent on the same wall 0n the floor above nor the basement below. Where was it coming from? We'd woken flea-bitten on our first morning (a gift from the animal sanctuary that had previously inhabited the place). Yet here we were, in the middle of ancient forest, in a house with space for ghosts to gather and new stories to unfold.

In dreams, my grammar-school headteacher, LC, appears with a tawny owl. They show up repeatedly, LC and the owl.

Held. Rest. Is it the owl speaking?

When I attended LC's funeral in 2007, returning to the church in Kirkleatham, her niece mentioned during the eulogy how proud LC had been that one of 'her girls' had been ordained at the first service of women's ordination. When my youngest daughter, C, and my son, S, graduated from their MA degrees at Teesside University in 2018, I took A. to LC's grave.

In the dream, LC smiles, one gold tooth, trim white hair, prim string of tiny pearls over a neat twin-set, belying imperturbable self-possession and wit. In the garden an owl calls into the night, her joyous *whoo* melding into sleep, hypnogogue and psychopomp.

When I married M, LC invited us for coffee, fed us rich Belgian chocolates, talked mildly of someone she had known — whenever she was with this friend, she told us, she felt wrong-footed…

She smiled, offered the plate.

M said LC had been talking about L's hold over me. I thought otherwise.

The owl is Cailleach-oidhche ghael — white old woman of the night, the knowing crone.

I listen to the night, drift back into the dream — in the ancient Welsh story, Blodeuwedd was transformed into an owl as revenge — she was cursed to become a harbinger of death because she'd chosen her own lover, didn't accept her lot. She wanted to be flowers, but even as an owl she couldn't be quelled.

Held, Rest. Is it LC speaking?

Metamorphic I

Mudstone to slate, flowers to owl,
we live with alchemy in this place.

Cwmorthin slate for a Roman fort, Tomen y Mur,
transforming the place of Blodeuwedd and Lleu.

Flowers for a girl to make him a bride.
Primrose, nettle and broom.
Mudstone to slate, flowers to owl.
Cockle and bean, meadowsweet, oak.
Mudstone to slate, flowers to owl.

Chestnut and thorn. She wants to be flowers.

Mudstone to slate, flowers to owl.
Flowers for a face, fair dexterous one.

She wants to be flowers;
                    they make her an owl —

y gofod rhwng merch a ddyn —
                    the space between woman and man —

Mudstone to slate.
Flowers to owl.

She wants to be...

On my writing room wall is a picture of a young woman looking into a mirror where she is reflected as an owl — part owl, part flowers, caught between states. Below her the legend: *I'm still here.*

In the dream an owl hoots, LC smiles.

I'm still here.

It's been an unseasonably warm October, allowing long walks in the forest. Now I feel a pull towards rest, but my work schedule from autumn into winter is a colour-coded riot on the calendar. Rest doesn't come.

My response to work overload is invariably that of Boxer's, the carthorse in George Orwell's *Animal Farm — I will work harder.* My reaction to being tired is to stay up till 2.00 a.m. catching up on writing or ordering supplies online for the house. I hear myself apologising for not doing more, ignoring the tension in my gut.

What am I doing here?

I came to the forest to change, but I brought myself.

In November, I find a teacher of alchemical herbalism. I don't want to be a herbalist who 'fixes' people so that they go on tolerating crushing lives.

And myself?

In the herbal course I'm facilitating, we each draw a body and on it the feelings and experiences of being this body, without adding words. My green heart is a knotted ball of string. There is an orange fire in my head, dry grey eyes, a scarlet fist in my stomach.

Rest, nurture, the plants of Samhain whisper —

burdock

valerian

centaury

broom

holly

sphagnum

madder

fern

mistletoe

yew

wormwood

sage

datura

yellow dock

banes

January starts wet and stormy, water bubbling up through the cracked concrete of the *sous-sol* floor, leaking in through the walls that dip beneath the water table until the basement runs with a fast stream, filling the channel my daughter's partner dug the previous winter, out into the field that has become a now-familiar winter lake where the Squiriou river swirls through our garden, breaking her banks in elation.

I journal in clotted drips, the contraction of midwinter, the garden waters rise higher. Words sparse and stiff until news of a death breaks the dam, words pouring out.

One of my herbal tutors suggests choosing a herb for each month, spending time with the plant daily. I write the list quickly, letting twelve plants tumble onto the page. I begin with plantain, spending time with her in the garden or forest, where she grows undaunted by winter, drinking plantain tea, taking a few drops of tincture held on the tongue, or rubbing her balm onto my skin.

Plantain is often used in first aid. A common weed, used for hundreds of years across cultures. The Anglo-Saxons held plantain as one of their nine sacred herbs due to her healing powers. But the point of spending daily time with the herb is to meet another being, to discover things I wouldn't find in herbal monographs. When we get to know a person we don't usually start by reading about them. Each day as I drink the tea or sit with the plant, I journal about where the herb travels in my body, whether the effect is warming or cooling, bitter or sweet, which of my senses are touched, how I feel.

For the first few days I experience what I expect, my mind already full of facts. I taste the bitterness that makes it helpful for the digestion, stimulating the liver to make digestive juices and astringing the gut, along with the coolness and moistness of the plant, attributes that make it soothing for the throat and lungs. Gradually I sense where the plant travels in my body — throat, lungs, stomach, but also lower, reminding me that plantain is an ally for the urinary system.

There is little change as I record my daily encounters until, on a day when I've been journalling about what I pay attention to, the same day the waters in the garden rise again, something shifts. It's the time of the dark moon and, as I listen to the owl hooting in the garden, I feel plantain cool every part of me, a refreshing wave.

In my throat is a cool elasticity. If you have ever picked a plantain leaf you'll have seen that her veins are like elastic threads, giving the herb the ability to bounce back when trodden on. My breath lightens and cools, throat soothed, airways cleared. At the darkest time of the month, I am held by this earthy, humble plant.

It is no longer me attending to plantain, but plantain attending to me. This stretchy, resilient herb, understands what it is to over-extend, to stretch too thin.

The next day, as I sit with a pot of plantain tea, the first cup feels familiar, but with the second a wave of grief washes over me, strong and disorienting. I weep with no idea why.

I'm so thrown that I run to my books — plantain as a digestive, a soothing demulcent, a wound healer... Nothing about plantain for grief. Plantain is not a nervine herb — not generally given for anxiety or sadness.

But plantain is a herb that moves the lymph, that moves the internal waters and quiets inflammation. Plantain is an antihistamine for watering eyes, but also moistens. Why wouldn't a plant so associated with lymph, water, the lungs, also act on the emotions? Water and lungs are intimately linked to grief. An understanding of plantain I would never have reached through books, internet searches, lectures...

Water energy surrounds me through January — the dark moon, saying goodbye to my daughter, C, after the midwinter pause (having not seen her for the previous three years and knowing it will be at least another two or three till we are in the same room again).

And then I crack a rib (or so I and my doctor believe). I'm tender with every movement, weak to my bones. I've stiffened over the winter, become unsupple. I make a salve of plantain, comfrey and daisy oils, essential oils of wintergreen and helichrysum.

Plantain's suppleness for an ageing human living in a crazy world where genocide is being daily redefined. A tender, resilient plant, here in a forest at the end of the world.

A heart beat away

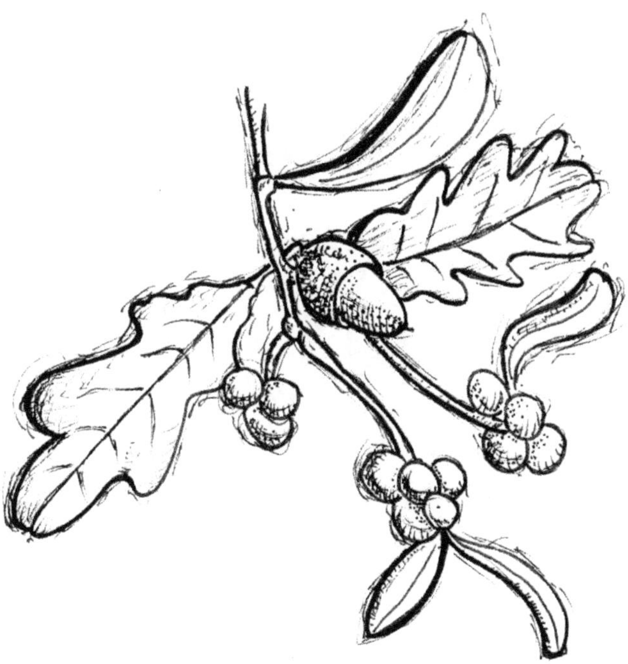

Always for the trance

I have been someone who falls into trance since I was small — a refuge from a house where money was scarce and emotion plentiful.

A house filled with the scent of burning coal, fried food and cigarette smoke. A house where three of my mother's younger brothers sought sanctuary. Sometimes one, sometimes all three — refugees from my grandfather's brutality. Five adults and myself (and later my sister) in a two-bedroom house. No bathroom. No indoor toilet. A place of raucous laughter that might quickly turn to argument or wailing above the chatter of the black and white television that remained switched on even if there was only the testcard to emit a whining buzz.

Trance took my senses inwards.

At the age of four I would make my way alone across Middlesbrough to my paternal grandparents' house. I'd set out from Longford Street towards Parliament Road, navigate busy traffic to get to Newport Road, bustling with lorries, buses, cars, people. My grandparents' home extended over and behind Comfort's carpet warehouse — long since demolished. The Canon Street end of the road.

I went most Sundays for lunch and sometimes on other days, when I'd walk with Granddad to the big public library. There were no books at home and my mother found reading unnerving in such a young child, constantly asking Nanna if I was 'normal'.

One Sunday I detoured across a piece of bombed-out waste ground around St Cuthbert's Church.

To a small child the building was vast and imposing, its stone blackened by the belching of heavy industry that all of Teesside sucked into lungs and skin. Large square tower, a hexagonal vestry and a stained glass window, a landmark that was finally brought down by Storm Pia at Winter Solstice, 2023.

That Sunday in 1965 I halted, drawn by music unlike anything I'd heard. My youngest aunts, five and seven years my senior, taught me pop songs, my mum sang Gene Pitney lyrics between bouts of weeping while she fried food, DG (one of my mum's resident brothers and in his early twenties) sang Irish freedom songs that my maternal Nanna would hammer out on the piano when enough of her brood gathered (nine of eleven survived), and EG (the youngest of the brothers, aged fifteen) had a penchant for TV jingles.

This new music was wholly other. Mesmerised, I walked through the stone archway, ducked round the thick wooden door into cool shade. Inside, light dripped through stained glass, puddling on altar and floor stone, rippling to organ music that left me aching for home.

Not the home I'd walked from.

Not the cosy, generous, smoky living room I was headed for, with food that was neither from packets nor fried, and conversation about politics and rights and horse racing…

A home whose location I couldn't name and had never visited.

Awash with the reds and blues, distantly aware of chords so exquisite they cracked open my tiny four-year-old heart, I stood gazing into fragments of light and listening to organ music… for a minute, for half an hour, for eternity?

Every muscle of my body relaxed.

When I blinked back into consciousness, nothing and everything had changed.

I returned to the church the next week, full of anticipation. The service was about to begin and the organist was playing music as people arrived. This was no one-off spell — I watched and listened, losing all sense of time or place.

On the third or fourth return a woman noticed me and swept me into the Sunday School, where I was given a tatty piece of paper printed with a bland picture from an improving story and told to colour it in.

I never returned.

But somewhere, at my heart's farthest edge, was home.

Weaving the stories

I started at Archibald Infants' School a term before my fifth birthday, a tiny scrap who barely looked three, appalled that my mother accompanied me on the first day. I walked alone from then on.

My best friend, MA, started on the same day. We both lived on Longford Street and I was the oldest by one day — I'd remind him of this frequently, causing him to bounce on me, which got him into trouble as he was so much bigger. We'd visited the school a couple of weeks earlier to look around the long Victorian corridors, huge assembly hall and rooms with high windows reaching towards the even higher ceilings. We'd been given tests to establish our reading ages — lists of words to be read out loud at a brisk pace, ruled into sections as the reading age rose. It covered the whole of the infant age groups, plus an extra two years (to test the more gifted upper infants). I read the whole card. A moment of silence was broken as my mother apologised for not knowing what to do with me. The headteacher smiled and reassured her — I would be fine.

I was a quiet child, reserved, logical, but never shy. On our first day at school MA cried for hours. When a bigger boy snatched the bucket he was filling in the sandpit, he wept louder. I stood before the offender, warned him never to do that again and pulled the bucket back. Not to be bested by a mere girl, and one so small, the boy tugged the bucket from me. It was at this point the teacher noticed, launching into a lecture on how boys should never take anything from little girls. He returned the bucket.

At school, there was order between the wonder of break and lunchtimes. MA soon made friends, enjoying kicking a ball with a group of boys. I had no interest or dexterity for the pastimes of girls — juggling balls against the school wall to the accompaniment of sing song rhymes or bouncing over a skipping rope. But, fascinated by the children, I'd position myself in a corner out of the wind and watch, drifting into trance, weaving endless stories from their imagined lives.

There was a day in the first few weeks when a boy from the Junior playing yard ran into the infant area to collect a stray football, noticed me standing alone and stopped.

Are those kids bullying you, Titch? he asked. I must have looked puzzled and he tried again. Won't the others let you play?

I shook my head. They'll play with me if I want, but I'm busy.

His turn to look confused. I explained I was making up their stories as I watched them.

Okay, Titch. Well I'm Adam and if they give you any trouble I'm just over there, right?

I nodded, smiled, added him to the story — a kind hero looking out for others. Even when they were fine.

The taste of sanctuary

On the outskirts of Redcar, aged seven, I found my way to another St Cuthbert's. A place with deep roots and traditions, built in 1763 on a site where a church had stood since 800, claiming lineage as one of the last resting places of Cuthbert, as his body was carried from place to place for two hundred years by the monks who fled Lindisfarne after Viking raids. A place of stained glass, where the organist played Bach with gusto and the interior walls looked like a Wedgwood tea service in grey-blue. It stood in a tiny village not colonised by the growing new-build estates of flimsy Wimpy houses where I lived. Unlike our estate, the village was tucked out of sight of the miles of industry that made up ICI Wilton and the newly nationalised British Steel, still referred to locally as Dorman Long.

The Sunday school had aspirations beyond colouring inside the lines and afterwards I'd stay for the Eucharist. I attended for the next eleven years, up to the day I was married there, aged eighteen.

It was half a mile and a world away from the family home where keeping quiet, staying still and not getting under anyone's feet could never compensate for being 'too clever'.

I was there for the trance.

At night my mother relived her childhood in loud nightmares of the sexual and physical abuse of her childhood. She relived her suffering and the torture of her brothers that she'd witnessed or heard. Scenes she would recount over meals, as she did the washing-up, or with her sisters around Nanna's kitchen table.

Only one of her surviving brothers was her father's son, others born to an American GI who'd moved in during World War II, promising to take them all to a better life. He survived war as a diver but died shortly after returning to the States, suffering the bends during a routine dive. My grandmother got a curt note from his family and, fearing destitution, took back her violent husband, exposing her three daughters, born when she was eighteen, nineteen and twenty, and her three half-American children, two boys and a baby, a girl, to a life of trauma, while she produced the next five children.

The 'illegitimate' boys were differently but deeply wounded. AG was cold and awkward, full of macho bravado. He spent long periods away as a merchant seaman. He talked about women in ways that made me shiver even as a child, and the woman he'd married had children to a succession of different men while he was at sea. But he competed for the love of his mother, a woman who had grown up in an Irish and Welsh immigrant family that had been full of love and music, that had not prepared her for the violence and disappointments that left her calloused.

The other, DG, was a tender bruise of a man who could fight his way out of any conflict and spent stretches of time in Durham prison. The family would joke that he was in E-wing. And though he and AG spent time 'back in the old-country' with Republican organisations whose songs we sang round Nanna G's piano at Christmas, his stretches were short — for stealing lead off roofs or doing arson jobs for the owners of struggling pubs and businesses in return for a cut of the insurance payouts. When he wasn't drunk he was a good cook, a whirlwind house cleaner, a sentimental dreamer who was kind to children. He died young, of alcoholic cirrhosis of the liver.

St Cuthbert's was a haven from home. A place for Redcar's intellectuals and traditionalists — at least those who also had a bent for religion. When I closed my eyes in prayer, another world opened — creatures that might never have existed, in fine detail and giddy colour, universes, faces and constantly moving light.

What they might be or where they came from was never the question. Sensations experienced in a beautiful place amongst safe people, tasted of sanctuary, smelled like home, sounded like a calling.

Discovering St Cuthbert's meant walking beyond my estate and into a country lane shrouded from the view of eighty square miles of heavy industry by the trees that lined the winding road. The hamlet that held the church was a fragment of an older place, complete with an old country estate, a scrap of woods, a cool-running brook, and a field of horses. Redcar has a long stretch of coastline that I loved to walk, but in this remnant of green, the birds sang louder than in our little back garden and sticklebacks flitted through the clear stream.

I am crouched alone beside the beck, a scrawny eight-year-old, two chestnut plaits reaching below my waist, a thin cotton summer dress, cloudless hot-blue sky dappling through trees lining the little bank, fingers trailing in clear water, gently stroking the wriggling sticklebacks that teem in the gurgling liquid. My dad's youngest sister has given me her well-worn copy of the *Observer's Book of Birds* and I chant their names as I sit by the stream.

sparrow

brambling

sandpiper

willow tit

skua

crossbill

thrush

tern

grey wagtail

robin

magpie

chiffchaff

blackbird

stonechat

redstart

warbler

gannet

The awkwardness of my body slips from me and an afternoon vanishes. Only a field away, a road runs, but I hear no traffic. Soon, even the songs of birds disappear. There is only water and air.

No one ever wondered where I was, though sometimes my mother would send me to look for my sister, five years younger, making her way as a three-year-old to the field of horses to stand, gazing in awe, finding the place of her own trance for a few short years before she was broken.

But for that while, both of us were there for the trance in a place a heartbeat away.

Life on the cusp

We inch our way up a steep gradient in an old Morris Minor Traveller that prefers to slip backwards, all of us leaning forward as though it might help the ascent. Wheels skid on the icy road, sleet slams against the windscreen. How long does it take? Time is suspended. We are somewhere on the moors heading for a nursery that has a rose variety my father has been hunting for. I'm eight or nine, J three or four. It's December and the daylight is folding into dusk.

Why are we looking for roses in winter?

Why so late in the day?

We're as frozen as time, as the car creeps forwards, whines and slides.

My mother rants and smokes.

J pulls the head off a doll.

My dad wanted to call her Rose — or Margaret like marguerite daisies. He wanted to call me Elisabeth. Instead we are Janet and Jane, about to fall off a hill on the Yorkshire moors.

My mother's protests get louder and I close my eyes tight, hear music I don't know the name of, see pools of red and blue light, the faces of strangers who make me their familiar.

Is it another few minutes or an hour?

A litany of the names of roses —

rosa mundi

phyllis gold

vanity

christopher stone

peace

celestial

henri martin

fragrant cloud

leda

superstar

felicia

old bush china

bourbon queen

louise odier

We don't fall.

My dad gets his rose — Fortune's Double Yellow — no more than gnarly little stems in a pot. They will be beautiful, precious, each pale primrose petal edged in deep pink.

I will give one of my daughters 'Elisabeth' as her middle name, and 'Rose' to another.

Some nights I'm still in that car, teal paintwork buffed between the ash framework, lumbering up the moors, time glutinous, the road treacherous. I wake, willing the car forward, willing the pilgrimage to end in roses, and there they are, their scent filling the dark.

Nanna Fortune died the next year. She was a strong, unfussy presence in my life. She and Granddad were hard-working, self-educated people who never made me feel awkward in my body. When my mother fretted volubly that I might be some kind of Midwich cuckoo because I learnt to read so young or was so self-contained, it was Nanna F who insisted there was nothing wrong with me.

I still have the once white, now dust-ingrained, service booklet from Nanna F's funeral, Psalm 23, which she'd taught me, on the central pages. She was not religious, but she loved language.

I was quietly enraged that I was not allowed to attend the service.

There was no goodbye. She'd been taken to hospital declaring she would never come home again and must have known about the cancer for a long time. A couple of days before she died, she was taken into respite care, which my dad mistook for convalescence, thinking she would be well again.

When Nanna F died, Dad asked if he could come to church with me. He whispered for directions all through the service — when should he sit or stand or kneel? He looked uncomfortable, but belted out the hymns in a loud and tuneless voice and told me afterwards that it was comforting. I was glad he'd found solace, but relieved that he didn't want to make a habit of sharing my sanctuary.

When Nanna F died, her old wire-haired terrier, Peggy, howled for days and my dad for months. He would wander the landing and stairs weeping until the crying became dry heaving that haunted the night. My mum took my sister into her bed, saying that the noise was disturbing J, but J was a deep sleeper. My dad haunted the house, keening, sobbing, sucking in air like a dying man before he slumped onto J's unused bed or sometimes…

When Nanna F died, I began having a recurring dream that still persists. Her house was an extraordinary space tucked behind and above the carpet warehouse. There were three rooms downstairs — the best drawing room, hardly ever used, the living room and a long kitchen. The upstairs rooms sprawled across the warehouse — five big bedrooms and a bathroom. In my dream there are many rooms in my Nanna's house — so many, lots of them hidden, full of what seems to be junk but turns out to be a world of resources, endless places of refuge. Whenever I have the dream I wake with a sense of lightness and, though she and Granddad only grew vegetables in their raised beds in the yard, the scent of roses.

A photograph of me. I'm nineteen or twenty, wearing a white broderie anglaise dress tied with a purple silk scarf at the waist, walking away from Cambridge market on my way to meet M for lunch. He took the picture as I walked towards him, my face the epitome of someone away with the faeries. I didn't notice he was there till I'd walked past him and he called my name.

Before he left, a retreat to a cottage by a lake.

Things forgotten: raincoat, matches, candles, self.

Hedges bloomed snow. Church squatted, tolling its bell.

Under ice, ancient gwyniad trembled above frozen silt.

Returning home: fungus in cups, sour food, stale bread.

Outside, the cherry tree blossomed early, birds sang.

Before he left, snow on Shrove Tuesday. Go to the precipice, said a friend, look over the edge, jump, plan how to land.

A moment after M left. Walking to the bus stop after taking parcels to Blaenau post office. A rare warm day, blue skies above slabs of slate mountain cradling the town. The sense of floating, picking up a thread of self I'd let go thirty-one years ago, aged eighteen.

Ecstasy, quiet and steady, enveloped me over and over in the next months — sitting in the Millennium Centre in Cardiff preparing to host a book launch, choosing Christmas gifts for my family, drinking in the views of Borth and Dovey Junction from the train —

beginning again.

Imbolc to Beltane

February 1, 2024…

In the night garden an owl hoots. The plump moon is waning, her light still a bright lamp in the dark sky. The house is quiet and I take a deep breath. Just past midnight, the first moments of Imbolc, an invisible threshold between the long winter and spring, each day holding a fraction more light than the last.

Imbolc is suspended between seasons. Winter is ebbing, despite frosts or stormy days to come. The time of turning inwards is giving way to the first green stems of snowdrops, tendrils of cleavers. Yet spring is still only a promise. The scent of the air shifts — sweeter, greener, but the sun remains low in the sky, the air chilled.

What is needful after the deep winter cold, after time spent in the cave of home?

Brigid, the saint of Imbolc, is associated with —

Hearth to return to for comfort.

Poetry to enliven after the sluggishness of the winter.

Healing from herbs that set the lymph coursing, ease the nervous system…

In the forest, new life emerges —

vervain

peppermint

watermint

cleavers

chickweed

birch

lady's mantle

primrose

verbena

plantain

nettle

dandelion

garlic

milk thistle

thyme

lemon balm

blessed thistle

heather

marshmallow

After the long January with the apparently cracked rib, longing to be more like plantain, flexible and resilient, I'm yearning for spring, but my body stays deep in winter.

I reach for vervain. One of the Druids' nine sacred herbs and a symbol of Awen (inspiration), vervain was known as the Enchanter's Plant, harvested at the dark moon, just before it flowered, with Sirius rising. It had to be cut with a sickle raised in the left hand. In Breton lore vervain was regarded as a plant of prophecy as well as inspiration; one of the plants mentioned in the ingredients of Ceridwen's Cauldron, the Welsh myth of how the bard and seer Taliesin was born.

A herbal tutor tells me everything in nature is language. A plant communicates through the shape of her leaves, the texture of the stem, her love of shade or sun, through colour, scent and taste, through the tactile, emotional and intuitive faculties. I spend part of each day of February stretching my senses towards vervain.

She is full of medicinal gifts — so bitter that the roots can cause nausea, but the bitterness makes her a tonic for the liver, promoting bile, stimulating the gallbladder and digestion. Vervain has an affinity with the nervous system and is a relaxant for the muscles.

Like the spring season slowly arriving, vervain's element is water. She will grow well in our swampy, boggy water-meadow and acts on the body's waters — stimulating milk flow in lactation, cooling headaches and hot flushes in menopause, helping the liver to clear hormones. Emotionally, vervain is not only sedative but helps those who need to let go, a herb that gentles us into relaxing.

But there is something untimely in our meeting. I feel like a friend has introduced me to someone she loves, telling me how much we will have in common, only to find myself wondering what she was thinking. Vervain feels cold. I've spent the winter craving warming foods, relishing hot cacao with chilli. I'm a winter hibernator. Cooling herbs can lend relaxation, but vervain stirs an ocean of chilling grief that I can't trace the source of.

Plantain had asked me to tend to grief, warned of brittleness that could make me liable to break. Asked me to become more supple.

Whatever vervain wants to tell me, I'm not ready to hear it. I have the disquieting sense she knows things about me that I haven't yet fathomed myself. Another time, we whisper to each other. Not now.

Sweet flag to see me through March while the rains continue. The mentor who introduced me to this gorgeous yellow iris told me a story of giving a few drops to a woman at a festival who had lost her voice — it was restored almost instantly.

When I was in ministry, voice was vital — conducting weddings, funerals, baptisms, celebrating weekly services, giving voice to the story of a community.

Until a series of workplace assaults ended that phase of my life, I was rarely sick. But if I ever came down with anything it was a sore throat — losing my voice forced me to rest. If I couldn't speak, I couldn't work.

Sweet flag (*Acorus calamus*) tastes like nothing else. There's a hint of sweetness, a strong, aromatic spiciness, slightly citrussy, and an undertow of bitterness. The powerful combination is followed by heat, a deep, suffusing warmth. She is the left hand of vervain and I fall in love, her warmth holding me.

Once sweet flag was used to make scented rush mats. The young flower stems (before the leaves unfurl) can be eaten raw in salads. The roots are nutritious, a flavour between sweet ginger and bitter spice, and can be candied and eaten to soothe the digestion.

My throat eases each time I take a few drops. One name for her is 'singer's root', easing vocal cords, numbing pain when the voice is exhausted, but also increasing the range and energy of the voice with a combination of stimulant and relaxant properties. A calming herb, helpful for those processing trauma, but not sedative.

A herb of trance. Each drop is a wave of energy, vital but quiet. Clairvoyance simply means 'clear vision' and I taste this clarity — of vision and voice. Yet she is also grounding and bodiful, good for stamina, her bitter principles boosting digestion, appetite, a sluggish metabolism. And I am centred in throat and gut instead of trapped in my head where I live too much.

My son, S, is the person in my life who reminds me that I am a body, that I can't be healthy if I get stuck in long ruts of work, nearly all of which is on a screen. When work or stress take over I become increasingly static and internal. Sweet flag joins with S to remind me that I am a creature. She roots me in time — *breathe into your body*, each drop insists.

Between Imbolc and Beltane — vervain, sweet flag and yarrow.

Last year's yarrow hangs in bunches over the kitchen table and at the window that looks onto the orchard. It's a May to midsummer herb of protection and traditionally wards off illness. Yarrow was also used for divinations and prophetic dreams, especially in matters of love.

Boundaries, he whispers. I know this about him before I begin taking yarrow daily through April. But it is only when I get to the end of April and reflect on the month that I notice how yarrow has shifted my perspective.

Yarrow is bitter on the tongue and a cooling herb, and although I've craved warmth since this incessant pain in my rib began in January, yarrow doesn't leave me cold. Unlike vervain, he's not a deep cooler of the parasympathetic system, and not sedative, but disperses inflammation. A herb who promotes movement — of blood, bile, digestion, of pain, wind, fevers and anything congested.

The rib pain persists, but no longer holds me static. *Breathe and move,* yarrow tells me each day. And, out in the forest, simply walking amongst the profusion of life as spring wakes, I feel more alive, stop clinging to an internal winter, think of the new season less as bringing waters of grief, more as nourishment.

Yarrow is a friend urging me to move gently, adding energy. I'm less reactive — that urge to reply to every email as soon as it lands dissipates. I diffuse yarrow essential oil — a rich green-blue from the presence of azulene, soothing, slightly moistening, an inflammation-regulator. He breathes out aromatic sweetness over a bitter base note. Here at the end of the world (Finistère is one of many 'land's ends') I breathe a herb of strength and boundaries.

Becoming defamiliarised has been one of the gifts of this move. I have been articulate since I was a toddler, but here I'm upended — a beginner in the language of the land I dwell on. The perspective-shift is disorienting and exciting, frustrating and expanding, and I am grateful for this stable ally.

Yarrow is a wound healer, his Latin name a nod to Achilles (*Achillea millefolium*), hinting at warrior energy, and a reference to how Achilles used yarrow to staunch blood and heal the wounds of his comrades. Salve for wounds, companion of the heart.

Mid-month I book a tiny wooden cottage by the coast for three days to mark the tenth anniversary of getting together with A. Work is suspended and the sky doesn't fall. Before we leave, I reach out to a wonderful writer to mentor this book. I've written novels, poetry collections, books on home education and autonomous parenting, and a book that dives deep into creative writing. But this is a new thing. Plantain has lent me its flexibility, sweet flag has opened vision and voice, yarrow is making me stronger.

The cabin at Plouhinec has a glass wall overlooking the sea. It's a place to read, cook and write. A place for walks along a beach of white sand backing into high dunes full of life —

sea pink thrift

wild mustard

hoary stock

three-cornered leek

buckthorn

capeweed

meadow buttercup

eland's sour fig

red clover

pink sorrel

bearded iris

dandelion

daisies

In the night garden an owl hoots.

In remembrance

Does it pass the placenta?

It's about your future, my parish priest, IF, had told me when I was twelve, before taking me to a debate about women's ordination. Acrimonious as that meeting had been, it did not prepare me for the journey to ordination in a church wallowing in misogyny. Early in my training, my grant was frozen while I proved that I could be a 'fit mother' to my unborn child. This was after I'd given up my income to train for ordination. In the second year, despite it being common for the wives of trainee clergy to attend tutor group prayers and chapel worship, babies and toddlers in tow, we were told that M was not welcome to attend tutor group worship with R, who was almost a year old.

When I was pregnant with my second child, my tutor let me know that in his opinion I had no chance of finding a post as a curate. And it certainly seemed unlikely.

The college principal has a friend who he's sure I'll 'click' with. But the parish doesn't have a curate's house and when the vicar learns we have no funds with which to buy one, he writes to let us know that, after all, this wasn't God's will.

A letter from a church in York is sorry to disappoint, but they couldn't possibly consider a working mother. They hope I will appreciate their concern for my best interests…

Love in His Name…

A Tory and Freemason. Yet Canon Pillsbury is keen to meet, says shared faith is all we need. I'm six months pregnant, go alone. He has a packed weekend planned, asks whether M is frustrated as a house-husband or simply an inadequate man.

I've invited people for drinks, he says, at 10.00 p.m. tonight.

I'm introduced as the one doing a PhD in feminist theology.

Contradiction in terms, dear girl, booms Red-faced man. Not that I have anything against you delightful girls.

I sip my orange juice.

And is your husband going to look after this baby too? an older woman asks.

Bit weird isn't it? Red-faced man demands.

He's got no choice, I say, I'm a feminist.

See! What did I tell you? Razor sharp or what? Canon Pillsbury laughs, gulps whisky, winks at me.

The letter offering me the post says my relationship to Canon Pillsbury should be thought of as a marriage — *with none of this role reversal nonsense.* He encloses a torn out sheet from the parish news in which he's written that his decision to offer me the post: *could only be likened to offering it to a very effeminate gay male candidate, because of the perversity of Jan's lifestyle.*

My pastoral tutor tells me he has every right to his models of ministry, says I'm silly to decline this post; urges me to reconsider.

Reader, I don't marry him.

And then I found P, who later became a bishop. My curacy with him was charmed and Rotherhithe was a place where I made lifelong friends. There, I completed my PhD in feminist Christology (during a maternity leave), breastfeeding C through late nights while I typed into an Amstrad 464 with a whole 64KB of memory.

But finding a second post after the curacy would prove even more difficult. Few parishes wanted a colleague limited by not being able to take the Communion service and unable to bless weddings. Women, at this point, were perpetual deacons, an order that men left after a year, moving on to priesthood and endowing them with a full range of usefulness.

After a long search, I found a place in a group ministry as deacon-in-charge of a sad church on a difficult council estate in Swindon. The congregation had dwindled. Often less than ten people attended a service, several leaving when I (a woman!) was appointed. The walls were moving apart, exacerbated by a ring of badly planted poplars that had sucked the water table dry, cracking the foundations of the church. It was damp, cold and was eventually demolished.

During my first Holy Week there, my local bishop appeared for an unannounced visit. I'd known PF and his wife when I lived in Bristol for six years after university. All of us active in the movement for the ordination of women. That day he looked round the ailing church and asked how i was doing. I tried to sound bright and hopeful and said something about the Good Friday services that week.

It's always Good Friday here, he replied. Don't stay in this place too long.

On Sunday afternoons, between the eucharist, celebrated with a handful of the faithful, and evensong, said by four or five of us huddled in the choir stalls, we would often go as a family to the stone circle at Avebury or to the arboretum at Westonbirt. The riches of the trees and flowers at the arboretum dazzled us, contrasting with the '50s council estate we lived on with its one green space — an expanse of neatly-mown grass between the estates of Parks and Walcott. Westonbirt was the first place we took S, a tiny two-week-old in a sling, with a woolly hat that protected him from falling chestnuts. At Westonbirt we walked in bluebell woods, sat under blossom trees, learnt the seasons of

ash

rowan

birch

spruce

sycamore

yew

lime

elder

fir

japanese maple

sweet chestnut

wild cherry

hazel

bladdernut

oak

incense cedar

beauty bush

hemlock

pine

walnut

beech

At Avebury I'd lay hands on the stones and listen to the silence — ancestors stretching beyond imagining — home to generations for at least six thousand years. What prompted people, 4600 years ago, to set up the imposing ditch and bank before erecting at least three circles of stones and the West Kennet avenue with over a hundred pairs of stones marching south from the henge? Once, the ditch may have been filled with water, giving the circles the appearance of an island. Thirty-six of the original one-hundred and fifty-four still stand. We don't know why the others were moved — perhaps it was related to crop and land management, perhaps it was an attack on 'paganism' by the church in the fourteenth century. But some stand still. Solid keepers of secrets.

Nearby is Europe's largest prehistoric mound, Silbury Hill, close to one of the longest long barrows at West Kennet, a Neolithic tomb for fifty people. We would visit these occasionally but it was Avebury that drew us, partly for the presence of the vegetarian restaurant there, set up by a group of archaeologists who had found it difficult to make a living and even more difficult to find good vegetarian food when they were away on digs. 'Stones' was creative and joyful and I still cook their recipes from two battered spiral-bound books full of quirky illustrations of the food.

We went to Avebury for nourishment — delicious lunches as treats eked out of our tiny budget or cakes on warm Sunday afternoons — but also for solace. While the children ran between stones, climbed the bank and rolled down it, I could stand with a hand resting on an ancient stone.

Once, at grammar school, a group of girls had played a game of giving one another a single word description. I don't remember L's word. Mine was 'serene'. My parents would have said 'away with the faeries'. My children still tell me I have 'a gift for oblivion'. Beside those massive ancient stones, sound and sight fell away, my body was light, cooler, rested. Elsewhere.

And afterwards, half in the world, my heart still light, we'd walk to the ring of four enormous copper beeches on one of the banks. I had no idea they were famous, that Tolkien had modelled his Ents on them. Between their knotted and exposed roots my body took on substance again, not heaviness, but rootedness. And always the same phrase — *linger, listen, connect, it is enough*. Years before, I'd been given a pendant as a birthday present, a titanium disc in purples with intertwined silver beech trees worked onto the surface. I imagined they were the beeches on the ridge at Avebury — symbols of connection. My youngest daughter, who I see only every few years since she began working in China, then South Korea, now wears that pendant, roots reaching across the globe.

In November 1992 the ordination of women was agreed by General Synod and in March 1994 the first ordination service took place. I was in that cohort, pregnant with my fourth child and, in the weeks leading up to the ordination, the centre of media interest as 'the pregnant one'. I fielded over fifty interviews in two weeks, hosting teams of journalists and photographers from Germany, France, Italy, Argentina… I still have the huge orange Le Creuset pot left on our doorstep by the journalist from *Deutsche Welle*, who'd offered money for the drinks and food we'd made for her and her team over two days, and which I couldn't accept. So she left the pot that's travelled with me for over thirty years. My other memento is a fat file of media cuttings. My favourite, from *Paris Match,* has a headline that reads *Ces Femmes Qui Font Pleurer Le Pape* next to a two-page spread picturing the women who made the Pope cry.

We visited Avebury a couple of months before the ordination to commission a chalice and paten from a potter who made ceramics featuring the copper beeches, the tree tops reaching beyond the rims of his bowls. On the underside of everything he made was inscribed: *For the joy of the sweet green earth.*

When we picked up the paten and chalice he had added an extra line: *let those who seek not cease until they find and when they find they will be astonished.*

Before the women to be priested left for a pre-ordination retreat we rehearsed the service in Bristol Cathedral, followed by a press-conference.

Three rows of seats, thirty-two in all, set out near the altar.

Do we have to kneel for all of this? one woman asks.

Yes, Bishop Barry's voice is tense.

What about Jan?

What about Jan? The bishop casts me a weary glance.

I'm fine, I confirm.

She's fine. Jan's fine! the bishop reiterates. Can we get on?

The third run-through is smooth.

The media are let in to jostle for positions at the photo shoot.

Are we ready? Bishop Barry twists to survey our cassocked rows. Sit up, Jan!

The woman next to me says, *S*he is sitting up, Bishop, that's…

I know what it is, thank you!

She grins and asks: Will you be ordaining Jan's baby, Bishop?

Don't be ridiculous! Ordination can't cross the placental barrier.

A gift to the waiting press, whose cameras flash.

On the eve of ordination, on retreat, I wrote:

And clouds
fall back,
winter trees
let go,
leave behind
naked pain
to bud,
and all creation
strains, drenched
in sap
that cannot
be refused…

Surrounded by woods, I drifted to sleep to the lullaby of a tawny owl calling me home.

Looks like carelessness

In October 1995 I lost father, mother, sister and brother-in-law.

> To lose one parent, Mr. Worthing, may be regarded as a misfortune; to lose both looks like carelessness.
>
> Oscar Wilde, *The Importance of Being Earnest*

They are, as far as I'm aware, alive and living on the Isle of Lewis at an undisclosed address, having cut off all family. They stopped communicating with me, their grandchildren, and my dad's remaining sister, who sadly died not able to make contact with him, long before they moved. They have similarly severed ties with all but one of my mum's surviving siblings. When my Uncle JF was dying he sent word pleading to see my dad before he passed away, but the call went unheeded. Later, my dad's sister, AF, went to Yorkshire to track him down, accompanied by her sons. They found my parents on a golf course where my mum warned them that if AF talked to Dad she would throw him onto the streets. They left, bereft.

My parents divorced decades ago, after my dad disappeared from his workplace in Algeria in the late '80s. Droves of working-class men, skilled and unskilled, went from the North-east of England to work in the Middle East after the '70s collapse of the industries that had employed tens of thousands of them. My dad had a series of contracts, moving from being unskilled and unemployed to earning large, untaxed sums. He was home for only a few weeks each year.

One Christmas Mum received a note on thin blue airmail paper:

Won't be coming home for Christmas, won't be coming home, CF.

Mum tracked him to the Philippines where he was apparently living with a young woman who had been working in the canteen in the desalination plant in Algeria where Dad had been based.

One morning about eighteen months later, while I was a curate in Rotherhithe, I opened the curtains to see Dad sitting in a hired car. He refused to say where he'd been, why he'd left, why he was back. He wanted a cup of tea, told me to ring Mum and broker his return.

Why did my mother take him back? An act of revenge?

When they were living in Darlington there was a news story one night of a man who had taken his wife hostage and was threatening to kill her. M and I were sure it must be them and rang the police for information.

It wasn't my parents, but over the next months, Mum cut the sleeves off Dad's shirts, repeatedly cut the plug off the TV, deadlocked doors when he left the house to buy a newspaper…

They remain together.

Occasionally, they would visit, my sister and her husband in tow.

J was bullied all the way through school, stopped attending when she was fifteen. A funny, curious, wildly energetic little girl became a depressed young woman suffering constant migraines. Her husband, RP, from a background of physical abuse, cut himself off from his family when he married. A skilful builder, hard-working and biddable.

They arrived one weekend when I was newly installed as a priest on an outer Birmingham estate. Dad placed a box of with several bottles of wine and another of whisky bottles into M's arms as they came through the door. Mum handed me a single bottle of wine, saying, The rest is ours, don't touch it.

They spent a day snarling at the children, refusing to let them watch their weekend cartoons and left the next morning (breaking their promise to take the children to Cadbury World), offended that I hadn't cancelled the church service to spend the morning with them.

They phoned soon after to say they would be coming the next weekend. I hesitated, said they would be welcome but I needed to talk about how we behave towards children in our home. My mother put down the phone. I have not heard from her since. They changed their phone number, moved house and, in the fullness of time, headed to Lewis, where they are not on the electoral register or in any directory.

In 2017 I was working on a book with a novelist, LW, who I admired greatly. He was Welsh, from a strict religious background and had a sister I'd met when we'd worked on his debut novel and warmed to. His name was an anagram of hers — Glenda and Landeg. LW was a scholar of African Studies, whose activism had saved lives, and a gifted poet and translator of the works of Luís de Camões. He lived with his Portuguese wife just north of Lisbon. He was a delight to work with. One day he phoned to ask if his novel might come out six months early. He'd had a terminal diagnosis and hoped to see the book into the world. He did — and I went to Lisbon for a single evening for the launch at Ler Devagar, an extraordinary bookshop in the LX Factory. In my journal I wrote:

> I have sat with the dying many times, but have never been so shocked as I was seeing LW tonight. He was skeletal. Only a year ago A. and I sat in the sun with him a couple of days after our wedding and we shared a bottle of white wine. He was robust, broad and hale, a confident, kind, intelligent man, full of vitality. I had to take a moment to convince myself I was seeing the same person.

LW was too ill to read at his launch, but I hosted the event, his sister read and a close friend gave a long and entertaining speech.

I was back on a return flight the next day, reading Kapka Kassabova's *Border: a journey to the edge of Europe*, writing quotes in my journal about the ways in which stories are composed of what we have lost and how we search for those losses.

Later, tired, standing on the platform at Manchester train station. I wrote:

> I saw my mother on a train. Just off the plane, standing on a wet platform, exhausted, and there she was, with my sister. Could two strangers look exactly like Mum and J? Exactly like me? Mum looked healthy — her hair cut in the style I remembered, but white now. J didn't look so well — pale, not so much overweight as watery. Tense.

Aunt MT had told me they were moving to the Isle of Lewis, which she'd learnt from Aunt EC, one of perhaps two people in the family my mum was still speaking to, though Aunt EC changed her phone number and had it listed as ex-directory soon after Mum left. I imagined Dad and RP were doing the removals while Mum and J took the train, which was heading up the east coast to Scotland.

As I stood, wondering if I was seeing things, my mother turned to look out of the window and we made eye contact. She turned to J and pointed, furtively. J shook her head and turned further into the carriage. The train moved off and I thought, *This will be the last time I will see my mother.*

The next day, in Hay-on-Wye for another book launch, I research the flora of the Isle of Lewis, write a litany of allies that will surround my family —

> beech
>
> eyebright
>
> field gentian
>
> birch
>
> bog cotton
>
> alder

primrose
bilberry
monkey puzzle
common twayblade
lodgepole pine
bog rosemary
machair orchids
sycamore
butterwort
red clover
lesser butterfly orchids
sphagnum moss
marsh cinquefoil
harebell
lady's bedstraw
hebridean marsh orchid
great yellow bumble bee
cross-leaved heath

I hope my dad's roses will thrive.

A red carnation

Life in the parish that followed Swindon looked like a picture-perfect story. The vicar with a stay-at-home husband, home-educating four bright children who took part in church life. We hosted dinners for parishioners, went to harvest festival barn dances as a family and were soon hard at work on an enormous and successful funding campaign to renovate the church hall and provide a local community worker.

My journal tells a different story. My relationship with M was threadbare. I regularly worked seventy-hour weeks while we failed to make ends meet and sank into debt. Though I loved what I did — the privilege of walking with people at birth and death, taking weddings and funerals, being a companion in sickness, curating the story of a community… I nonetheless longed for a life without unsustainable expectations and an income that might support us.

On Stir-up Sunday, November 23, 1997, my agonising over how to make changes was superseded by life. I returned to the church after the morning Communion to pick up a hymn book, intending to write the rota of future weeks' hymns. As I approached the church door a voice behind asked, Are you the vicar? I told the pale, thin young man I was, not expecting him to pull out a knife, instruct me to open the church and lock us inside.

Trance shielded me as he waved the weapon. I have no soundtrack of what happened. My memory is a silent film. Ordination may not pass the placental barrier but love does. When I was doing my PhD one of the delightful discoveries I made while exploring feminine language for divinity was that in the Hebrew book of Jeremiah, specifically chapter 31:20, the words in God's mouth about 'his' heart longing for his people and being filled with compassion have the same etymology as the word for 'womb'. God's womb aches for their loved ones.

Cocooned in silence, at knife-point, time losing form, my body still breastfeeding my youngest child, leaked milk, and I wondered what my children would remember of me if I didn't leave the church alive.

The young man left with his sports' bag heavy with the takings of the autumn fair the church had held the day before. Most of it was in coins gathered from the tombola, guess-the-weight of the cake, crafts and other stalls.

I collapsed onto the floor of the vestry, eventually aware of being ice-cold and the sound of banging at the church door. When the flurry of police activity and obligatory press-conference subsided, a friend lent us a holiday house near Oxford for a few days. Afterwards I returned to work. Cards and donations poured in for the church and praise was heaped on me for carrying on as normal.

In a sane world only Boxer, the carthorse in George Orwell's *Animal Farm,* could have been proud of me while I pushed on, but I was in a world where 'service' had taken on an unhealthy sheen. I was no longer in trance but deep in shock. And on I went.

The second assault was a public spectacle. A man who had absconded from a local psychiatric hospital came into the church after the Easter Sunday service and asked to speak to the vicar. The church warden's wife pointed me out and he approached, grabbed me, calmly explained that his daughter had been taken by aliens and the only way to get her back was to go through death, but he couldn't go alone. A vicar would have help from God, so he needed to take me with him. He roared at anyone who tried to approach. A couple of members of the congregation stayed in the building, not approaching, while the rest left. Eventually I noticed police officers, low to the ground, snaking down the side aisles, and was able to occupy the man in conversation about his daughter as the police made their approach and freed me.

The shock of the first assault had begun a pattern of bouts of mastitis — milk crying out in my body. I started to have pelvic pains and cysts were found. When we took a holiday in July, at a friend's cottage on Dartmoor, I developed a fever but felt nothing but the deepest cold during a heat wave, hiding under layers of quilts, shivering.

I journalled about not returning to work, but it was our only income and tied to our shelter. I took sick leave and slept through a month, the Rural Dean and Archdeacon both phoning to ask M if I was 'actually ill', the Dean warning him that diocesan patience with me was wearing thin. By then I was seeing a consultant for the breast issues. Under the constant pressure of mastitis the milk ducts were widening, rupturing, becoming clogged and calcifying. I was seeing another consultant about the ovarian cysts. My GP urged me to leave the church, while the hierarchy dispatched the Diocesan Women's Officer to advise me to return to work promptly or lose my stipend.

The third assault was fast and minor, but left the most physical damage. The boy, probably about fifteen, surprised me as I was setting up a mid-week evening Communion. The safe was locked and the keys nowhere visible. Panicking and seeing nothing of value, he picked up a large demijohn that was used to collect donated loose change and threw it across the vestry, pushed me hard and ran. I fell into broken glass, lucky to avoid the larger shards, landing on an outstretched hand that was peppered with glass splinters. The real injury was to my spine, which took the impact of the fall.

I tried to keep going, my working hours becoming longer, more frantic, but the pain radiating down my arm grew worse until I woke one morning unable to move. Fogged with Tramadol and in a neck brace, I spent three weeks immobilised before forcing myself back to work.

That summer, 2000, I led a pilgrimage to Iona for a group of twelve parishioners.

I had not been on the island since I was twenty-three, a charmed week when the abbey held a feminist theology retreat and a question had been posed at the end of a walk around the island's sacred locations: *what are you doing here?* I'd left early on the 6.00 a.m. ferry after watching the sun rise over a ruined shepherd's bothy on the shore. I was heading to the wedding of friends — M's best friend who had been our best man, as M would be for IS, and a friend of mine from school, CG. We'd introduced them.

It was the first time I'd seen L since before my own wedding, five years earlier. We smiled and acknowledged each other.

I always knew you'd look good in Laura Ashley, she remarked,

After the wedding we house- and cat-sat for IS and CG while they were on honeymoon and I invited L and her husband to dinner. They arrived with their baby, H, in a Moses basket. H slept the whole evening. We made polite conversation. And I have not seen her since.

Did we hug goodbye?

On the trip to Iona in 2000 I thought a lot about L and how she'd seen my marriage. Before the assaults, I'd been journalling about leaving M. But after the attacks, there were days, weeks, when the effort to look functional, to go on maintaining shelter and income for my children, was beyond exhausting. And I was losing faith. On Iona, I tried to write myself into rekindling both faith and love — with M and with God. I protested too much, failed to convince:

> I find it hard to imagine life without the rhythm of ritual, the sense of transformation that faith has given me, but I can't find the god I've attended to since I was four years old, the god I've credited with all that is good. This god is absent — not a wilderness absence, one of those god-shaped holes that palpitate with presence — but an absolute nothing. It's not like the sudden lack of a sense — losing the sense of smell, but a matter-of-fact ordinariness that this thing simply is not. That there is no gap to be filled.
>
> But how can I leave this group of people, whose stories I've articulated? I love them, don't want to hurt them or burden

them with my doubt. But don't know how to go on stringing their words together — preaching, presiding over liturgy. It has always been an act of storytelling, a story I've believed. I haven't lost faith in life, but the source of this story has vanished.

If God was a gap in my vision, where was M? On Iona I wrote love letters I never sent and knew to be lies, trying to coax myself back to some feeling. But the distance between us was as great as my distance from a god whose existence I couldn't remember.

I returned from Iona to cycles of work and collapse that continued until November that year, when I visited my GP to ask for a week's sick note, reasoning that a short break would give me the energy to rally for Advent and Christmas.

She simply said, You don't really think you are ever going back there do you?

All Soul's Day. The bereaved arrive to remember those they loved. The names are read and, one by one, candles are lit and, on the white altar, a red carnation laid down for each name. In remembrance of...

Outside, the November air is as sharp as glass.

Winnie says, I won't forget this service, the most moving All Soul's of my life.

I shiver, look back at the church. Inside, candles burn on darkened sills and red carnations wilt in remembrance.

I won't forget this service or ever step inside this church again.

Tŷ Meirion

We bought Tŷ Meirion with a lump-sum from the church after my medical retirement. It needed serious renovations and had no kitchen. We moved in April 2001, just before Beltane. S was almost 7, R 14 and T and C, 13 and 10. It was the first time they'd lived in a house that strangers didn't walk into, that parishioners didn't regard as an extension of the church.

The novelty of privacy, as well as a view across river, fields and granite was an instant balm. It would be years before the mastitis would (mostly) abate, before I would learn how to manage the injury to the spine so that it wouldn't flare, before the fatigue would lessen to a rhythm that I could anticipate and manage. And in that time I'd learn a new landscape that nested in a new language, though my Welsh would remain basic.

Return to Tŷ Meirion

I want a house — secluded,
a place to keep the chaos
out, a granite womb:
slung against slate,
hills; the sound of birds
hurtling to stake their claims,
while wind intones its lullaby.

We become so used
to fractured days,
to weeks spent

keeping one step
ahead of the rains;
to months when all we can do
is mend the fence,
then mend the fence,
then mend the fence;

to endless years when
it is enough
to name the things
that anchor us —

this photograph
of a younger face,

this picture book
that I read to them

a thousand times,
this yellow shell,

this scrap of slate.

I want this place —
a foot on the crumbling earth.

When I'd begun the process of leaving the church, the question of whether I was 'actually ill' was raised again. Medical retirement would give me a small pension without which we'd soon be adrift. I am forever grateful to the doctor acting for the Church of England pensions board, whose name I don't know. He told the board firmly there were no questions to be answered as soon as he received documents from my GP and the three consultants I was seeing.

We had a breathing space to renovate the house and for M to find work. First we needed a kitchen. And the house needed stairs between the ground and middle floors, which had been taken out to make a flat for the previous owner's mother. For over a year I cooked on a camping stove in what would become the study, washed pots in the hand basin in the corner. We ate at a blue plastic camping table. The ground floor had been gutted and had a concrete skim over the foundations. The kitchen took eighteen months to construct and, to eat in it, we would walk out of the front door, around the house to the back door (the house, tucked into the hillside, was three floors at the back, two at the front). It was another year till we had the stairs in place and the corridor they sat in was still unfinished when I left in 2020. While the kitchen, stairs and a downstairs bedroom were being constructed, T slept on the sofa for almost three years. Slowly the house became liveable — the shelves in R's room done nine years after we'd moved in, the floors finally sanded by S, long after his dad had departed.

The feeling of temporariness lingered for years, added to by the unfamiliar land and a new language. But after M left, neighbours regularly gathered around my table, came to bale us out during several house floods and were ready with practical help.

Before then I slowly learnt the land, let the mountains, Moelwyn Bach and Moelwyn Mawr, breathe me in, walked the lakes' edges — Llyn Ystradau and another at Cwmorthin, the abandoned slate mining village above Tanygrisiau. I watched for chaffinch, hawfinch, robin, waxwing, warblers and swifts, listened for the tawny owl that called the stars to shine and the moon to fill. I spoke flora and, like the plants, thrived on thin acid soil, drank in perpetual rain, listened as the place whispered welcome and resilience to injured flesh and bones.

heather

rowan

sundew

gorse

bluebell

welsh poppy

snowdon lily

rhododendron

purple saxifrage

common mallow

alpine chickweed

mossy saxifrage

moss campion

roseroot

himalayan balsam

fir clubmoss

broom

alpine meadow rue

green spleenwort

thrift

dog violet

Violet to breathe us through grief, heather for luck. I gathered sprigs to fill the tiny study — the new home of the infant Cinnamon Press. It can't be done, Jan. You can't just start a press, I heard repeatedly from M, but though I was still far from well, I needed some foot in the world. Cinnamon began with a poetry magazine, each copy printed and stapled in the little study. An anthology of poetry from

Welsh writers working in English, for which I got a Welsh Books Council grant and, miraculously, a slot at Hay Festival. A literary competition financed our first two solo poetry collections, one of which was short-listed for the Forward Prize for Best First Collection. Twenty years later we've published hundreds of books — poetry, novels, short story collections, memoir, creative non-fiction, mixed genre… Cinnamon is a not-for-profit — it's never been 'gainful employment', but it has been and is passion and purpose…

Tŷ Meirion was tumbledown and quirky, but offered sanctuary in a dramatic, beautiful place. I fell in love with quiet, slate, gorse and heather, a landscape of long recovery.

frog orchid

foxglove

starry saxifrage

butterwort

alpine saw-wort

fly orchid

globe flower

brittle bladder fern

wild angelica

marsh orchid

fen violet

glasswort

shepherd's purse

bugle

tansy

bladder campion

navelwort

spear thistle

eyebright

hogweed

dyer's greenweed

Beltane to Lammas

May 1, 2024…

In April yarrow whispered pauses into my life and I began to experiment with afternoons writing in our local café-bookshop in the forest. L'Autre Rive is a remarkable place of vegan cakes, good coffee and herbal teas, tables nestling between shelves of books, an impressive selection of herbal tomes, as well as radical politics, poetry and novels (in French, *naturellement*) and a few books in English.

I try to gentle myself away from the mantra of *I will work harder* to *I will live from home*. I can't encourage writers and those seeking wellness to pause while I push myself relentlessly. Rhythm — always it's in the rhythm. In one of her letters Virginia Woolf wrote:

> Style is a very simple matter: it is all rhythm. Once you get that, you can't use the wrong words. But on the other hand here am I sitting after half the morning, crammed with ideas, and visions, and so on, and can't dislodge them, for lack of the right rhythm. Now this is very profound, what rhythm is, and goes far deeper than words. A sight, an emotion, creates this wave in the mind, long before it makes words to fit it; and in writing (such is my present belief) one has to recapture this…

In life as in writing.

When I find the rhythm it's a revelation — quiet and profound — but over and over it slips away. I need to tend it each time, the way a candle flame needs tending in wind.

At each of the Celtic festivals I exchange a gift with A.

This Lammas I give A. an art book by Angela Harding — *Wild Light: a printmaker's day and night*, and he gives me a book in return

— *Derek Jarman's Garden*, along with a card he's painted — bright yellow cowslips. We sit in bed with mugs of herbal tea — a calming blend of fennel, chamomile, yarrow, meadowsweet, lemon balm — poring over the books before a breakfast of yoghurt, berries, seeds, nuts. I'm practised at making myself breathless with pace but this morning I work without rushing, then walk in the forest — flowers partying, leaves every shade of vivid, birds ebullient with song, and an early purple orchid in the hedgerow beside the brook.

crab apple

plantain

mountain strawberry

red campion

creeping buttercup

daisy

dandelion

meadow starwort

nettle

yellow archangel

bugle

herb robert

forget-me-not

wood speedwell

primrose

water dropwort

bluebell

bittercress

foxglove

dock

comfrey

lesser celandine

violet

early purple orchid

In the evening I read the whole of the Derek Jarman in one sitting — it's sad and beautiful with gorgeous photography by Howard Sooley. A place that came from terrible illness, yet birthed such beauty and joy. And the plants — growing in wind and salt on rocky soil and thriving —

helichrysum

fennel

artemisia

angelica

poppies

dog roses…

For the second week of May I'm in a little apartment in Crozon — a week of silence and solitude in which to write. The flat is further from the sea than I'd expected, but walkable. I'm restless, spend the first evening re-organising a website to distract myself, before reading a book on visible mending.

The next day my laptop begins to do strange things. Emails take several minutes to load, I can't save documents or copy sections from them and can't upload audio files. The day vanishes as I tussle with fraying technology and I arrive at an online yoga nidrā class frazzled and overwhelmed. To heal we need to de-escalate our nervous systems, my guide says.

Out in the garden in the evening, the moon is a Casilda-sickle. My heart slows into the spaciousness. There is quiet. There is time.

A long walk the next day. The coast is dramatic — impressive boulders, swathes of silver and golden sand. The sun high and bright, flora preening in the warmth —

valerian

rosy garlic

climbing fumitory

cowslips

thrift

silver ragwort

sea heath

milk thistle

yarrow

heather

pink briar

gorse

stonewort

dune thistle

The walk back is steep and energising. The computer loses more function each time I open it, but, with hours of remote and patient help from A., I manage to write.

Crozon is a place of vivid dreams — the recurring dream of my Nanna's large and sprawling house. In her bedroom are little doors, less than three feet high, that open into a triangle of loft space. They are painted dark purple and become passageways to other worlds — marvellous, colourful, safe. *In my grandmother's house are many rooms.*

Over lunch I read a post by a writer who is remembering her mother, full of poignancy, loss and love. She ends with a call to get in touch with our mothers if they are still alive, tell them how much they are loved. I've just been writing about how I have not spoken to my mother for twenty-nine years and realise I have not one memory of ever being held by her. She must have held me as a baby, but would talk about how she'd leave me in the pram screaming, waiting for my dad to come home. Profoundly unmothered herself, abused by her father, she likely had postpartum depression. How could she find her way to warm touch, to intimacy with a daughter, when being a girl had been so dangerous for her?

I weep for both of us, but most for her — still out there, nursing her hurt as rage. I was mothered by my dad, who would walk the house with me, miles round that tiny, cramped space, with its poky rooms, trying to quiet a crying baby who would hardly feed. I have been grandmothered, other-mothered, met in dreams by ancestors, adopted or otherwise, rocked to sleep by owl-song, held by the whispers of plants, cradled by trance.

I was born in May, and on each of my birthdays in France so far I've gathered hawthorn blossom and leaves from the beautiful tree at the entrance to the forest opposite our house. I ask permission and leave a gift of honey. As I gather, sharp thorns stay concealed under frothy blossom.

This May I spend time each day with hawthorn — visiting the tree, taking drop doses of the tincture, drinking her tea. I don't find the scent of hawthorn's flowers deathly, despite associations with the plague due to the smell of death being compared to its blossom.

For me the scent is musky and sweet, full of desire. Hawthorn is a herb of the heart, a guardian tree. Once, branches were hung over house doors for protection, including from lightning. And in France there were many spells for healing with hawthorn. The fragile-looking flowers and bright leaves make a delicate, refreshing tea, an astringent undertone, a hint of sweet nuttiness, a light, floral note.

Hawthorn is complex. She has her thorns, her strong boundaries, warnings of dire consequences if she is cut or taken from without permission, and yet she offers healing. And always she asks:

How is your heart?

What does it take for you to listen to your heart?

I've loved her since I was a three-year-old, carrying armfuls of blossom into my Nanna G's house, only to be told, vociferously, Get it out of the kitchen! You'll bring in bad luck!

She is such a familiar plant that I can forget to listen deeply. It's easy to see what I expect. The folklore is part of this familiarity — associated with Christ's crown of thorns and with resurrection and the famous Glastonbury Thorn, which flowers twice a year, reputed to have sprung from the staff of St Joseph of Arimathea. Hawthorn adorned the altar of Hymenaios in ancient Greece, was carried in wedding processions and has Celtic associations with Beltane fertility rituals and hand-fasting.

The first drop doses — a tincture of flowers, leaves and berries — go to the heart — always the heart with hawthorn. Slowly, through the first week, the tincture travels to the gut, the kidneys. In the first week of May, I journal what I already know.

A wonderful herb for circulation, strengthening heart muscles and veins, balancing blood pressure. Full of nourishment, she lowers cholesterol, reduces inflammation in blood vessels. She works healing on the digestive system and regulates the metabolism. Hawthorn assists the kidneys and a tea of her leaves and flowers makes an excellent gargle for sore throats. She is also supportive of the joint linings, synovial fluid, collagen, ligaments and vertebral discs and is a relaxant ally — relieving heartache, easing anxiety, promoting sleep. She has an affinity with the female reproductive system — regulating blood flow, boosting libido and fertility and, during menopause, calms hot flashes and night sweats. But most of all she is a herb of the heart, tendering us into rest, mending what is broken, soothing what is bruised.

This year the blossom comes and goes quickly, but for a short while she is lavish froth and foaming sweetness, scent of sex and desire, uninhibited and mischievously impolite, a mass of brilliant white boldness, thrilling, joyful, casting pearly petals to the breeze in abundance. Over the month, hawthorn enters my dreams. Or is she dreaming me?

I think of *The Little Prince*, the book I've loved since L introduced me to it:

It is only with the heart that one can see rightly; what is essential is invisible to the eye.

By the second week of May, taking a few drops of the tincture, my gaze softens, body and heart settle into another time... a childhood moment on an early summer day, sweet-scented with heady May-blossom and a song from school assemblies running through me;

Sing a song of May-time,
Sing a song of Spring;
Flowers are in their beauty,
Birds are on the wing:

May-time, play-time,
Earth has given the May-time;
Thank her for this gift of love—
Sing a song of Spring.
Blossom on the hedgerows,
Sunshine on the hills;
O, the happy May-time
All my being fills.

The moment elides into another... as a young mother with toddlers — a field surrounded by blossom trees, hawthorn petals on the breeze as we sing rhymes — *row, row, row your boat...* May mothering, hawthorn singing. I have been grandmothered, other-mothered, met in dreams… And I have mothered.

On the tongue the melding of bitter and sweet, strong, almost syrupy, tonic and warming... I am held and mothered, sleepy, a snippet of song that played at junior school parties, the year we did exams before secondary school that would separate us into the 'clever' and 'not-academic' — a couple of months before my eleventh birthday... Johnny Nash's 'I can see clearly now' with its insistence that the bright, sunshiny day is ahead. A song I have not thought of in decades and only know one verse of.

The next day drops of hawthorn melt my edges, heart and body. Where do I end? Where does the owl hooting softly in the heart-filled night begin? The soft light in the bedroom greens, hums, mild warmth of the herb surging and singing in me, I am *seeing with the unworn sides of the eyes,* as Thoreau put it, dropping deeper and deeper into a heart suppled by hawthorn, my breath, her breath, our breath…

settle, open soften…

On the forest track, white blossoms weight the branches and then they are gone.

June begins in a village just beyond the small town of Plougasnou, a week to walk, write and read with A., a gift for my sixty-third birthday. The cottage has a tiny conservatory with a view over the bay, framed by a huge cedar tree and the warm stone of the neighbours' house. A. and I eat there each evening while he listens to the story that I am slowly excavating…

Hélène, who takes care of the lovingly-tended house, has left jars of wild flowers in every room. In the kitchen, a jar of plump oxeye daisies. On the table in the covered veranda, where we eat watching the turquoise water rise and fall around pink granite rocks, a 1930s emerald La Loraine glass of tall white daisies cosy with pink valerian. I'm spending time with daisy each day of June.

As the evening sun whitens the sky we head for the seashore —

rocks

sand

pebbles

kelp

pink granite

shells

waves

We climb the headland, sea on both sides, June flora lavish — elder offering great saucers of frothy cream, oxeye daisies, tall and joyous, foxgloves dripping magenta and mischief, pennywort towers and hairy-legged Queen Anne's lace. The headland, emerald fern and red campion, mauve frills of thrift swaying to the waves, plantain raising long stems heavy with seed, the sea turquoise and cobalt —

sorrel

buttercups

bramble

white clover

honeysuckle

dog rose

valerian

violet

While A. clambers rocks to take photographs or make quick sketches, I linger with the plants.

rosemary

campion

self-heal

vetch

lavender

cranesbill

vervain

stonecrop

hawksbeard

poppy

cow-wheat

tree mallow

sheepbit

wild radish

calendula

And everywhere common daisies and oxeye daisies, wide-eyed, following the sun.

I am back with L on the school playing field making daisy chains, winding them round our wrists or wearing them as crowns — protective magic.

This year the daisies are more abundant than I can ever remember. When we get home the little orchard is a field of oxeyes, their smaller cousins crouching low to the grass between them.

sheepbit

moon daisy

calendula

dog daisy

bellis perennis

oxeye daisy

banwort

leucanthemum vulgare

marguerite

english daisy

bairnwort

bone flower

common daisy

llygad y dydd

lawn daisy

bruisewort

Between the unseasonal rains of June I gather daisies. Simply collecting these flowers, joy fizzes through me. They are infectiously buoyant — so much so that it's tempting to go on gathering more and more, to keep harvesting the cheer. I thank the plants and drop the flowers into a bowl of water to macerate in the sun, keeping some to add a tangy note to a tea.

The flowers have a buttery texture — full of saponins, a chemical that is a natural soap — not only cleansing but wonderful for coating delicate membranes, like those of the respiratory tract. *Bellis perennis* are not often thought of as medicinal plants, but make a powerful cough syrup. The leaves of oxeyes are peppery and delicious. The crushed leaves of daisies work on bruises, as strong as arnica, but without the ecological stress. Daisies help with chills, boils, jaundice, wounds, scalds, rashes, tuberculosis, sore eyes. They are tonic and their bitters promote appetite, relieve constipation and intestinal inflammation, support the kidneys. Daisy is helpful for joint pain, arthritis, gout; known as a bone healer. William Turner referred to daisy as banwort or bone flower.

Daisy has an affinity with the female reproductive system. Oxeye daisy is *Leucanthemum vulgare*, and is beneficial for leucorrhoea, balancing oestrogen and relieving menstrual cramps.

But it's the simplicity of daisy that has made her a symbol of new beginnings, associated with Freyja, the Norse goddess of love. Her links to cycles and fertility date back 4,000 years and have connections with childbirth. In some Celtic traditions, if a baby died, daisies grew as signs of consolation.

When the flowers have macerated, I strain the essence and add brandy as a preservative, though vinegar or glycerine could also be used. Mother essences are gentle, subtle preparations taken in drop doses. I take the first drops before sleep, joy bubbling up. A few drops deepen breath, a life less bruised. My inner twelve-year-old whispers me back to a self who had so much time. *Sit amongst the daisies. Savour. Shh.*

By the third week of June, daisy has eased deeper, quieting the pain in my rib. *Sew and mend.* She travels to heart, lungs, pelvic bowl — cool-lulling, grounding, softening senses so that my pre-teen self flits through dreams for the rest of the month. She wears a white crimplene dress with a tiny patch pocket at the breast, embroidered with a pale blue flower. Her long plait is messy and she is tiny — thin and easily taken for a girl of eight or nine. But she has an unselfconscious assurance. Like daisy — belief is her gift.

At the Summer Solstice, I launch my new novel, *smiling at grief in a house in a forest where life grows.* I mark the event with A. and my son, a group of gracious friends and strangers at L'Autre Rive, the café that is also the setting of the novel.

Reading it, I realise I've always known that high sun and sorrow, joy and grief, are inextricable from summer. In the June following my eighteenth birthday, a couple of weeks after taking my A-levels, I secretly packed my belongings, hiding bags in cupboards, ready to escape my mother's rage, anticipating her ultimatum to leave home. In the June after my forty-ninth birthday, our almost thirty-one years of marriage ended. M moved out and our divorce would follow in the next June. In our first year in Finistère, A.'s dad died at Summer Solstice. It has taken me a long time to realise that this turning point of the year, the fires of summer, have always filled me with joy and yet left me dazed with melancholy.

Get out of your shadow, daisy and my inner twelve-year-old whisper. *Sit amongst the daisies.*

I listen, walk in the forest, get out of my shadow.

What am I doing here, in this forest in a country so far from home?

There is no clear answer, only that this too is home, that this is a place where writing and herbal practice might meld into something tender and generous.

July begins grey, wet and windy. In the forest —

sheepbit

moon daisy

calendula

yarrow

yellow pimpernel

bird's foot trefoil

marsh thistle

bittercress

cock's foot

hogweed

valerian

loosestrife

dog roses

royal fern

enchanter's nightshade

nipplewort

And then a month with mugwort.

An uneasy month, dull and damp for the first three weeks before switching to sweltering heat that explodes in more rain. The forest is shrouded in wet veils and I bake lemon cake — comfort food for washed out days.

Work is unremitting and the news as heavy as the weather — good friends and family facing cruel illnesses... my oldest daughter assaulted three times over the last few weeks — strangers on the street or on trains confident they can attack a trans woman with impunity. I wish I'd told her to put a piece of mugwort in her shoe before setting off to Barcelona on a sweltering day — en route to a political conference in France.

Herb of protection.

As I sit with mugwort, the moon is almost full.

horse moon

hay moon

claiming moon

thunder moon

I taste thunder in the humid air. Mugwort is *Artemesia vulgaris,* named for the Greek goddess Artemis, a hunter and lunar goddess, associated with wild animals, wild places... Outside the tawny owls call. Each night through July I rub infused mugwort oil into temples and pulse points before sleep. A moon goddess herb for dreams that are vivid, strange, but not disturbing.

I want this house to be a dreaming place. But in the midst of an uneasy month, fretful for a perilous world, anxious for loved ones, overwhelmed by work and a mountain of paperwork for house renovations... I work into the night, drowning in tiredness,…

It's mugwort that calls me back to a dream of growing, tending, creating in this scrap of forest…

felon herb

st. john's plant

chrysanthemum weed

wild wormwood

Old uncle henry

chinese honeysuckle

maiden wort

cronewort

Known in the Middle Ages as the mother of all herbs, mugwort is also a herb of the womb, kidneys, hair, throat, blood. She eases period cramps and childbirth. A remedy for menopause symptoms, reducing the frequency and severity of hot flashes.

Maiden and crone, blood and womb. I'm reminded of discovering how Biblical translations glossed over the shared root of words for compassion. *My womb yearns for my people*, God might say in an alternative translation.

I talk to a trusted herbalist about a circulation problem in my right ankle. It's built up over the summer and she points out that the pressure point for the womb is exactly where my circulation issue is most troublesome.

What is my womb telling me?

As I race between tasks, time feels breathless…

I walk in the forest, carrying mugwort… lose myself in the cool air, already sliding towards autumn though it's only late July. Foxgloves droop, bowing out slowly, colour fading. Butterflies ride the breeze,

dark green fritillary

brown argus

speckled wood

red admiral

gatekeeper

violet fritillary

cloud yellow

wall brown

small heath

idas blue

silver-washed fritillary

Along the verges the first wood betony of the year and bugle in the long grass and everywhere

dropwort

campion

hogweed

nettles — bearded with seed

Further along the path, my skin beads with the wood's humidity, oaks lean in. The river, iron-rusted, flecked with foam, lollops seawards, singing. And I slow… every pore drinking in chatter of birds, forest and river, mugwort calling me back to this forest, asking again —

What are you doing here?

By what we listen to

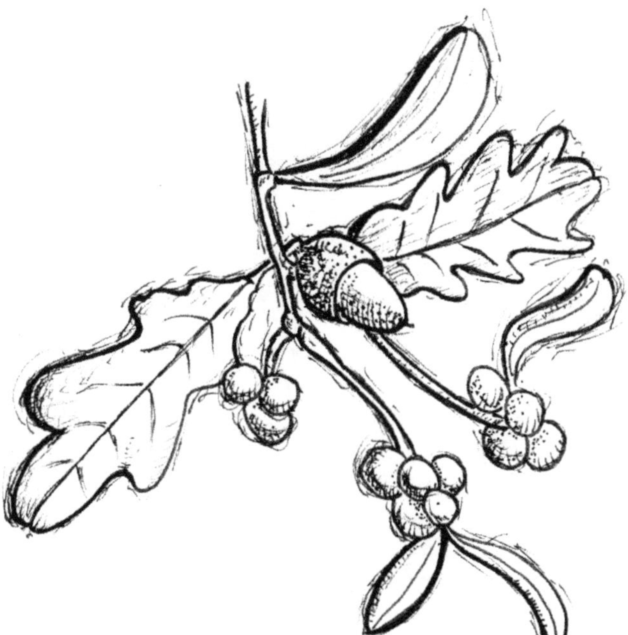

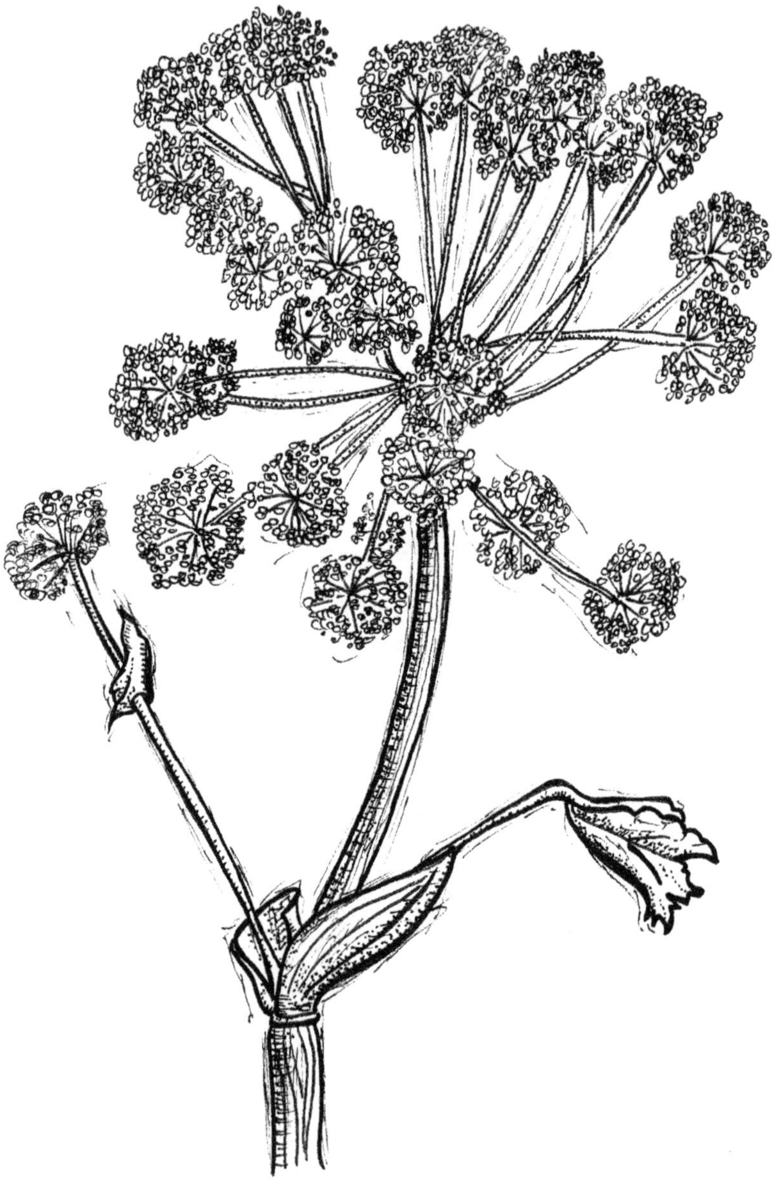

A foot on the crumbling earth

When I wrote my part of the collaborative poetry collection, *Slate Voices*, I imagined I was writing about place — the history and land of a ruined Welsh slate mine above the village where I lived. At the launch, surrounded by those who knew me well, I realised that beneath their surfaces, the poems charted the slow death of a long marriage, that those who had gathered were holding me as I emerged from the trance of writing a crumbling life. It came as an epiphany that almost stopped me reading.

> Cwm
>
> We come over the lip, drop to the bowl where lake seeps from itself, heather underfoot, a monkey-puzzle tree beside the house. Lichen enamels walls that close round memories, dust. No one speaks. The water can't recall the smell of sweat, the taste of blood, the words for slate—the path to the chapel is long.

In the years after founding Cinnamon Press, the mastitis occurred less frequently and I learnt how to take care of my spine so that it only occasionally left me immobilised. Fatigue remained, but I could become more hands-on in home educating. Insomnia was constant, but late nights allowed me to complete an MA in novel writing and a debut novel that was published by the now disappeared Bluechrome Publishing.

When I read my journals of this time I am shocked by the *Through the Looking Glass*-life in which logic and truth were perpetually reversed. None of the communication between me and M seemed to bear any relation to our existence. Confused and exhausted, I questioned my grip on reality. I was brittle, overwhelmed, rapidly gaining weight. To talk of separation was proof I was a hard, cruel person. What kind of woman shatters a marriage after thirty years?

I don't remember why I walked down the aisle aged 18, the texture of the vows on my tongue, the way the shaft of light on the altar's starched white linen made me shiver in my cream polyester dress.

I first contemplated separation three months after we were married. I had bronchitis in my first term at university and was sent home. M was still working at ICI, Teesside but would join me in Cambridge after Christmas, starting a new job there. He had a flat in an ugly ground-floor block near Albert Park in Middlesbrough. There was a mattress in the bedroom with old tea-chests as bedside tables. The living room had an ancient TV and a couple of sagging floor cushions. The place was musty and gloomy, but I slept most of the time. We had not lived together for more than two weeks since our hastily-arranged wedding and every atom of my body told me I was in the wrong place with the wrong person. Exhausted from weeks of coughing and fever, I woke groggy one morning and told M we had made a terrible mistake. We should part before this went any further, before he moved to Cambridge. His look was louder than words. To leave him was impossible, unbelievable, not going to happen.

Thirty years later, sheltering in a world of trance, the message was unchanged.

On a dark winter night when rain poured like waterfalls, an argument whose details and illogic I can no longer recall became so intense that I fled the house. Drenched and shivering, I walked towards the abandoned mines at Cwmorthin till I ran out of light, tears and rain mingling.

Cwmcerthin

Cwmorthin: from Cwm-certh-hin:
cwm for valley;
-certh for awful/dangerous;

-hin for weather.

Darkness on the face of the earth,

a litany of awfulness:

Mae hi'n bwrw glaw,

It rains

mae hi'n cesair,

It hails,

mae hi'n eira.

It snows.

Mae hi'n arllwys.

It's pouring down.

Mae hi'n chwerw ac ddiflas.

It's bitter and miserable.

Mae hi'n mellt a tharanau.

It's thundering and lightning.

Mae hi'n ofnadwy.

It's terrible.

Mae hi'n tywyll.

It's dark—

over the face of the deep —

Back at the house I huddled in the coal tunnel rather than go in, staying there till the cold became a bone-ache that drove me inside. R wrapped a towel round me and refused to leave me alone with M.

I'm going to run a bath, I said eventually. And R shepherded me out.

When I returned to the bedroom, where M hadn't slept for more than two years, he told me we would talk — properly.

Belief is my gift, perhaps my curse.

I waited.

Finally, I asked when we were going to talk.

That look.

He had said what I wanted to hear. What else could he do?

I'm deaf in my left ear and sometimes it blocks painfully, but the earache that followed was deeper, more persistent, didn't shift with lavender oil or heat. Each day, the pain built, my hearing shutting down. It snowed in late February, cold pressing into flesh. When I finally saw the doctor, we talked about menopause, of how life-long low blood pressure had shifted to hypertension.

That May I was 49. The girls sent gifts from Northampton and Hereford. R gave me Folio copies of Elizabeth David's cookbooks and S gave me a cardigan speckled with knitted daisies. M left a book on the Welsh dresser — an old copy of *The Leopard* (a book I already had), its pages and cover eaten by mould.

Everything must change so that everything can stay the same, Lampedusa writes, his Prince convinced he can ward off change by manipulating it to his will.

Later in the day, S gathered a bouquet of wild flowers for me.

I began thinking of ways to move out with R and S, aware that with the house in negative equity it would force us into bankruptcy. On desperate days, I looked at vacant posts for parish priests, but even had I been sufficiently healthy, bankruptcy seemed preferable.

In our last winter together it snowed heavily and we climbed from Tanygrisiau to Cwmorthin lake, the ruins of the slate mine blanketed in icy whiteness. Sitting by the water, time melted, there was only lake, snow, the one remaining cottage, its roof near collapse, its ghosts looking out to glimpse the couple we might have been.

We carried bleakness into New Year. And then an unlooked for miracle arrived — a friend offered me a large loan for an indefinite period so M would have the funds to leave. An offer of unassuming grace from someone I had known for only a few years, someone I liked enormously, but had spent little time with. Her generosity changed my life…

M was due to move out while I was in Gardoussel in France, teaching a writing course, but his landlady changed her mind after M had moved his boxes into the attic studio of her house. I wept into the night.

Late in June, M found another place to live while I was staying with a friend in Cardiff to attend the Wales Book of the Year Award. A Cinnamon poetry collection won — *I Spy Pinhole Eye*, by Philip Gross, illustrated with pinhole camera photography by Simon Jenkins.

M gathered glasses and forks from the kitchen and left without saying goodbye to R and S.

At the beginning of July I set off with R and S on holiday, leaving the house empty while M returned to collect more belongings. The holiday house sat at the mouth of the river Teign, and we were joined by T with her partner F, and C and her boyfriend. There were boats for the river, a sauna, exquisite countryside and, for the first time in over twelve years, I slept as soon as I lay down, and without waking through the night. Insomnia had begun with the assaults, but had never left. I assumed the sleep was a one-off, a mark of exhaustion, but I slept the next night and the next, insomnia melting away.

Avalanche of grief — and yet…

I felt infinitely light that week — beside a river in spate gentled by the plants on the shore.

liverwort

shepherd's purse

dog-pelt lichen

elder

evening primrose

sand-hill screw-moss

tree lupin

foxglove

dune brittlestem

sea rush

wood anemone

wild garlic

red campion

Everywhere red campion. Hardly used in herbalism, yet inflammation modulating, giving back voice, astringent for wound healing, soothing kidney supporter, washing away what needs to flow. *Silene dioica* — in folklore a plant —

of the heart

of rituals to clear emotional obstacles

of protection and healing

of starting again—spring in July…

Everywhere red campion.

Pause savour let go

Single for the first time in my adult life.

To simply walk down Blaenau Ffestiniog High Street on my way home from the post office was bliss.

Recently a friend wrote about the experience of 'walking without questions', the state of getting out of that anxious nervous system loop of internally asking ourselves 'what if…'? It struck me that my trances are the opposite of trying to solve things with an over-active, over-thinking mind. I was walking without questions that warm blue day in Blaenau. I travelled without questions to book launches, falling into beatitude on trains so that I came close to missing my station many times.

The blessings of trance rubbed against the grief of letting go of the hope I'd clung to for three decades. And between these poles was the wonderful mess of daily life.

When M left, we'd been running Cinnamon Press together for five years. I had never maintained a website or designed a book cover or used the software on which the designs relied. My impaired vision doesn't allow me to drive and I lived in a tiny rural village.

There was no lead-in time for learning, but the generosity of others was miraculous. Neighbours offered lifts to the post office, boxes of books piled high in their classic American station wagon. An author asked what I most needed, then persuaded a friend to build Cinnamon a new website while he and I learnt to maintain it, giving me skills to eventually do the process myself. My youngest daughter helped me learn design software and designed some of the book covers, despite having a heavy load of her own for her Fine Art degree. My oldest daughter, R, worked with the press part-time to lighten the load of editing. Authors volunteered copy-editing skills and another author offered a venue for writing courses in the cottages around his farmhouse, tucked into exquisite countryside near Conwy — the beginning of a long collaboration.

I learnt to ask for help.

Those years were the last of my calling myself a home educator. It had been integral to my identity for two decades, writing books about both home education and living consensually with children. R was about to begin a PhD, T had been working as a paediatric nurse since graduating and C was at university. S turned sixteen at the end of the summer after M left and started OU undergraduate courses that autumn in lieu of A-levels. I needed to withdraw my territory — marriage, home educator, an overly-mothering mother…

And someone carrying too much weight.

I'm less than five feet tall and had ballooned to someone with 30kg to lose. It took more than two years, every kilogram the weight of a wound.

And as I let go, we also engaged in a long process of tracking down what might be happening to R, who'd begun having sensations that appeared to be neurological. Eighteen months later, R was diagnosed with Multiple Sclerosis.

Letting go of any pretence that we control what life brings.

One of the poets I'd worked with across most of Cinnamon Press's history, Omar Sabbagh, who has known deep challenges in his own life, sent me a poem. He was one of the many people observing a metamorphosis. And for this I am forever grateful:

A Small Bird, Burning

It started with Muscles.
My scaffolding, my furniture
And all the outside world for
My mind. Echo of an echo, I stood. I bowed.

The sand-hued heap of body
Was the arc beneath the altar
At which I worshipped.
No covenant therein.

My language was only religious
In that meaning was tongue-tied
Fibres, bunched tight for the rites
Of I, me, sire and sire, decreasing myself...

Now that's all locked away, shelved,
An old ornament in my continuous soul —
That bright fiction!

In the upturned bowl
Of my palms, I've a few letters
I'd like to let loose to fly:

A small bird — Faith — burning.

Gather listen tender

Lammas, Lughnasadh, Harvest…

For large swathes of two years during the Covid pandemic, gathering was something we couldn't do in person. We learnt to gather in other ways, online and by messages… Yet more and more, in a fragile world, we thirst for connection.

Who is the teacher? my religious studies and philosophy teacher, JS, wrote in my school report while I was studying A-levels. He had been a Methodist minister, but found himself crushed by the narrowness of thought. No room for his 'question everything' approach and maverick views. We debated Anselm and Aquinas, Tillich and Leibniz as I ferried messages between him and my concerned evangelical vicar, who was afraid that theology would rot my faith. But it was neither theology nor the series of assaults that ended this faith journey, rather the shock when those in the hierarchy turned away.

JS was a listener. So too was LC, my grammar school headteacher and English teacher at A-level.

On a grey, wet day in the fifth term of sixth form, she came with news that I had passed the entrance exams to Cambridge. I was writing poetry to while away time in a history lesson. Each lesson with CR, a kind teacher close to retirement, read to us from the set text, assigned the chapter for us to make our own notes for homework, then would read the chapter to us again in the subsequent lesson. It was easy to get ahead, leaving time to sit at the back, lost in trance, writing screeds of unthinkably awful (but formative) teenage verse in faux-Romantic style.

Lost to the room, I startled as a hand settled on my shoulder and there behind me was LC. She asked CR if she could borrow me, smiling to herself as we walked to her office.

Well, you have more going on than even we realised, she said with characteristic honesty when we reached her office.

Was she talking about the poetry?

Apparently I'd not only impressed the examiners with my theology, but had written a stand-out essay in the general paper: *The greater the art, the worse the society. Discuss.* I remembered not having the faintest idea where to start, believed I had no hard knowledge to offer, so decided to enjoy myself, riffing off the theme for three hours. What I lacked in public school cramming I made up for in having nothing to lose.

I was going to Cambridge as an Exhibitioner, which meant they would pay me a tiny bursary.

Between the euphoria of that day and beginning university, was a wedding.

Unlike my friend GMS, a comrade from the sixth form debating team and now a KC, I didn't join the Union at Cambridge. M found my confidence in debates 'too much'. And, despite seven years of drama and elocution lessons, numerous Eisteddfods and choosing university over drama school, I didn't join Footlights, Cambridge's famous drama society. Also 'too much'.

But my joy in every lecture and supervision was unquenchable. If JS had introduced me to the subtleties of philosophical and theological analysis, my new tutors were building a cathedral of questions. Coming from a house with no books, bar the horse racing almanac and those I'd bought with pocket money, having never drunk coffee that wasn't instant, or tasted cheese that wasn't dyed orange and mass-produced, Cambridge was an Aladdin's cave on an alien planet. I was entranced.

From my first day at school, everything beyond my front door — school, church, L's home — had been another world. Cambridge was a magnified version. I made friends, discovered vegetarian cooking, learned mediaeval dancing and jazz ballet, wrote three essays a fortnight, danced at May Balls, saw Shakespeare and the heart-breaking *Abelard and Héloïse* performed in Clare College Gardens and fell in love with the river Cam, Granchester Meadows and its flora.

willow

early marsh orchid

buttercup

water horsetail

marsh marigold

creeping jenny

ragged robin

spike rush

plicate sweet grass

fennel pondweed

marsh bedstraw

vervain

enchanter's nightshade

thorn apple

holly

strawberry clover

fat hen

poppy

But it was a double existence…

My relationship with M was volatile, my sense of self rapidly eroding. A couple who lived beneath us, in the Victorian villa turned into college flats, befriended us, never hinting at what they might have heard through the floor. SDM was deep into a PhD. SDF, a brilliant mathematician, took on their cooking only to find every vegetable was in revolt.

What will be the best thing about completing your PhD? I asked SDM one evening. Having time to do the cooking, he replied.

So I cooked for them while they provided friendship, though they would have done so without any transaction.

It was years before I realised how many angels in disguise had listened without me having to say a word.

In my second year, I learnt New Testament Greek with a supervisor at Newnham, together with three compatriots also struggling with the language. Another young woman from Selwyn and two young men, from Robinson and Corpus Christi colleges. The others had come through the public school system — expensive educations and the assurance of belonging. The tutor scented my difference and was happy to let me know I was an interloper. The translation I'd just provided was wrong, she insisted one day. I was puzzled, sure I'd decoded the sentence correctly. But it was not my Greek that was at fault. My English phrasing betrayed my background. Why were Cambridge colleges allowing my 'kind of people' into this hallowed institution?

I rose, told her she was an obnoxious person, and not even a good teacher. I would leave now and not return. My shaken comrades eyed each other, then the quietest stood and said he agreed, followed by the others. The leaving was euphoric. I walked down Grange Road on a cloud until I heard someone calling my name.

JPMS was my director of studies. When he'd interviewed me I'd entered his study to find him on the floor hunting for something lost. He had an air of absent-mindedness that belied his deep scholarship and deeper compassion. Now he paused on his rickety black bike having noticed me, having sensed… I collapsed onto him in tears and he listened. Within a few days he found me not only a PhD student — Christian, a Benedictine monk — who would teach New Testament Greek to our band of four, but also a university counsellor.

Graduation came and, with it, labyrinthitis. I was too dizzy to walk with the cohort leaving Selwyn, had to be ferried to the Senate House in a car. At the moment of the degree being conferred, two-rugby playing vet students took me under the arms and deposited me in front of Owen Chadwick, Master of Selwyn, whose quizzical look burst with the unasked question of what might be going on. Despite a day of nausea and photos in which I look grey and unsteady, it was a momentous occasion, even when M's mother, RW, declared that I had deliberately spoiled her day by being ill.

I'd hoped to remain in Cambridge for another year to do a postgraduate certificate in education, but M and his mother had decided on a move to Bristol, where RW was living. Their relationship was fiery and unstable and RW despised me, despite enjoying boasting to friends that her daughter-in-law had just graduated from Cambridge.

Unanchored, I found new friends on my teaching course and in the local church congregation, where the vicar was another Selwyn graduate. I joined the local branch of the Movement for the Ordination of Women and a group campaigning for justice and equality within Christian institutions, the Christian Parity Group, led by MD and RD, who had been Principal of the Methodist theological college in Bristol and served as President of Methodist Conference. An ecumenist, teacher and academic, he and MD were committed to racial and gender justice. In all of these groups I was the 'baby' but never condescended to and, when I began my PhD in feminist Christology, RD became my unofficial supervisor and adviser alongside my excellent supervisor at Exeter University, AHBL.

RD died a month before my youngest child was born in 1994, but gathered with me and others at my ordination service at Bristol Cathedral in March 1994: RD and MD, together with IF, the parish priest who had told me, aged twelve, that debates about women in the church were about me; my headteacher, LC; P, the priest I'd been curate to in Rotherhithe, who would become Bishop of Taunton; JC, priest and also later bishop, as well as a close friend from theological college; N, the rector of the team ministry I was part of in Swindon, and other dear friends.

Along the path so many have simply listened. Increasingly I include the more-than-human world, especially plants, in this. It's an act of attention to listen in return. Writing in *Gravity and Grace,* Simone Weil compared attention to prayer. No doubt my notion of prayer differs from Weil's but I share her sense of recognising another creature.

Thoreau talks about looking with the unworn sides of the eyes. Listening to plants, a gaze passes between us, profound as love, an encounter that asks the senses to open beyond words. Plants are Other — the Thou to my I — inviting me to step beyond myself for the merest instant that seems to last forever, returning me to the world with memories on the edge of forgetting.

What calls to you? The ocean, a mountain, a particular animal…?

After the work-place assaults in the church, I could only describe my former faith as amnesia. It had blazed bright since I was four years old, entranced by a stained glass window that admitted me to otherness.

And then it became impossible to reconstruct.

But still the owl calling into the night and the wood violets in the garden are holy. And still I know how to attend to the trees and plants in the forest.

What we tend to, what we turn towards, gives us away. And if absolute attention is prayer, we make the world more sacred by what we listen to.

The writing on the wall

At the end of a thirty-one-year marriage, the deepest grief was the loss of hope. From the first flickering cave paintings or hand prints on cave walls, we have reached out, saying 'I was here'. I had placed my trust in the wrong place as a naïve eighteen-year-old and persisted in doing so for three decades.

For my fiftieth birthday my daughter T gave me a beautiful necklace — the sort I would never buy for myself — a teardrop emerald on a fine gold chain. It was the year after I'd separated from M, a few days before our divorce was finalised and T gave me this gift in case I never had someone in my future who would give me something special.

A little over two years later, in August 2013, I met A. He attended a course I was teaching at Tŷ Newydd, the writer's centre for Wales. His mother had died a few weeks earlier and he was a quiet participant, but we paired for the ice-breaker on the first evening and there was something reassuring and intelligent that made me write in my journal that he would be a friend.

In November A. attended another course I was teaching — a biannual event co-hosted with a friend and author who ran a holiday cottage business around his farmhouse. I had spent the previous week on tour with an Argentine poet and his translator (a Welsh writer and academic). It had been exhilarating and exhausting and now I'd be teaching full-on, mornings, afternoons and evenings, as well as cooking for a group of writers, some who returned to the course year after year, some new.

On the second full day we walked to Eglwys Celynnin Sant at Llangelynnin. One of the oldest churches in Wales, the current structure was built in the twelfth century over a sixth century foundation on the site of a more ancient holy well. Entering the remote building I realised it was Remembrance Day, the anniversary of the last service I'd ever conducted, and there was a wash of sorrow for a faith I could barely reconstruct.

> I don't know how long I stood in the cold stone interior, a trance of images — carnations, candles, a chalice held high, *Do this in remembrance...* the broken promise of *I will ever sing to thee...* Until the cold revived me, drew me outside to November sunlight, low and mild, towards the healing well where my colleague PM stood in his own trance, remembering the last walk he'd taken to this place with his brother, who'd died soon after.

In the evening workshop, sharing our work, PM would recite the poem of how he wished he had dipped his brother into the well, bathed him as he had when they were young.

On another day the group walked into the hills. From the high vantage, PM pointed out where the Romans had landed and made camp on what had been an iron age fort. There had been a hilltop village where we stood, but now only the broken walls of a forgotten dam and a small windswept lake.

Each of us wandered with our thoughts, A. and I arriving at the broken wall together. Decades ago, when the place had been inhabited, there was a day when the mobile cinema arrived further down the valley. The houses emptied for this annual treat. No-one was home when the dam broke through the wall, flooding every building. Not one life lost.

A. made a remark about 'the writing on the wall' which had not worked out so well for the Chaldean king, Belshazzar. I replied with a misquote of Daniel's message to the king: *weighed, measured, found wanting*. As A. laughed, the slightest glance passed between us.

And then he walked down to the lake.

That evening we each shared a piece of writing we loved, I read C.D. Wright's 'More Blues and the Abstract Truth' and A. told me the title was from a 1964 Oliver Nelson jazz album.

On the last day I did a one-to-one session with A., exploring his writing, which I loved. And on the final evening, after the group had shared extracts from their own writing, we sat up late, talking books, art, film… both of us devotees of Béla Tarr and Andrei Tarkovsky.

And so began a correspondence that grew ever more intricate. We began emailing about the novel A. was working on and that I was mentoring — long emails. Singing along to Joan Armatrading as I painted the living room before Christmas, A. was in my head. So I was delighted to receive a beautiful hand-made Christmas card from him.

We met at Birmingham Museum and Art gallery in early March, ostensibly to talk about the novel. A. brought me a pamphlet he'd published — a short story that — 'full disclosure' — revealed the level of anxiety he lived with. I walked with him to the train station before going on to another meeting and, as his train pulled out, I booked a trip to Bruges for his birthday in November. We hadn't spoken about a relationship, but if nothing came of it… I'd still go to Bruges.

We began exchanging books as well as emails — I sent poetry to A., he sent Konrad Beyer's *The Sixth Sense.* I sent Anne Carson's *Nox,* he sent links to music with recommendations for more music and films. We wrote of the small intricacies of our days — the cooking, packing to go to launches or to teach another course, helping C with her MA application, A.'s brother's new job, making bread…

> *16/03/2014, 23:39*
>
> Thinking about those nagging doubts. It's hard to get to Virginia Woolf's ideal of 'rapture' with writing — so much easier to listen to the inner editor/common sense (I've always been suspicious of common sense — Nabokov advises we shoot it.) I did a session on that with the writing group here at Tŷ'n y Coed today — using lines from a Carver poem (Afterglow) as prompts for continuous writing. It's a whole other level of consciousness to apply this type of flow to creating a piece of art…

One email a day became two, became… shared references layered between events, discussions of what we were reading, theories of the universe… Staying in York while visiting S, who was at university there, I came within a centimetre of flooding the bathroom, running a bath between going back and forth to the bedroom as we emailed in real time. My children telling me — *Of course you're in a relationship.*

I invited A. to visit in May — to cat-sit while I was away with R as well as some time together with the pretext he'd teach me a layout design programme.

We wrote 'love' not 'best wishes' at the end of emails, along with Jake Cave — an anecdote from A.'s family based on a childhood misreading of his mother's handwriting — 'Take Care' had looked like 'Jake Cave'.

At the beginning of April A. added a scene set in Bruges to his novel, *Vitus Dreams* —

> *01/04/2014, 18:58*
>
> Have you ever been to Bruges? I haven't — but I've had a hankering for it since seeing *In Bruges* — and now it's in Vitus too — here's to one day visiting a *F****** fairy tale city.*

We met again in mid-April for lunch in a noisy Italian restaurant in Birmingham and afterwards I began sending him E E Cummings poems —

> 13/04/2014, 00:24
>
> In honour of Cummings and because I used this in my PhD in feminist Christology (which took some working in), but most of all in honour of new places…
>
> somewhere i have never travelled…

And a couple of days later —

> *15/04/2014, 19:56*
>
> Weird question for a Monday.

> I've got a launch in Paris in September — I've found a little apartment and have various young people coming with me — R, S and R's friend, JM — a week of museums, Paris walks, and haunting Shakespeare and Co.... Do you want to join us?

And then —

> *16/04/2014, 18.46*
>
> Yes — a beautiful friendship and, more and more, it occurs to me that something extraordinary is taking shape — so in the interests of honesty and bravery, and to mangle a quote from *Annie Hall* — a relationship is like a shark. If it doesn't keep moving forward it dies. I think we've got a live shark on our hands. Hoping you might think so too, but it's not a threat...

By the time A. visited in May it was as more than a cat-sitting friend. A couple of weeks later he joined me for a launch tour for the poetry collection *Slate Voices*, written as a collaboration with Mavis Gulliver.

A. proposed in July, came on holiday to Menton with me that month, to Paris in September and Bruges in November — the trip I'd booked on the station after our meeting in March. He moved to Tanygrisiau in May 2015 and we married in September 2016, two years and five months after the shark email. Five years after telling my daughter, T, I would never marry again. It was the wettest day I've ever known, a memorable achievement after fifteen years in North Wales.

We began with a tiny 'legal' wedding at Dolgellau registry office, where we walked down the aisle to Sidney Bechet's 'Petite Fleur' performed by Philippe Audibert, a busker we'd met in the Marais in Paris. Then to a hand-made ceremony in Blaenau Ffestiniog, in a friend's house that had once been a chapel. Family and friends gathered from Wales, Scotland, England and Australia. A close friend, AC, from the days when I was a curate in Rotherhithe, presided. Another friend, V, an extraordinary costumier, made my dress and her son, JM, who'd been with us in Paris when we got engaged, made a cake covered in roses. We bought finger food, juice and Prosecco, roses in blush and cream that my daughter's partner, F, fashioned into bouquets and button holes — a forester, and the only one of us with the dexterity for the job.

My son, S, was our photographer, my youngest daughter was A's 'best woman' (she and A. in pink). My daughter, T, and a friend from Cephas days, K, who had travelled from Melbourne, were my best women, in shades of blue. K, who had been my bridesmaid when I was eighteen, and A.'s dad, Ming, were our legal witnesses. My oldest daughter, R, son, S, and A.'s brother, did readings, a Cummings' poem of carrying one another's hearts and a passage form Rilke on the wonder of living side by side, guarding each other's solitude. The speeches were extemporary fragments from anyone who wanted to speak. This marriage would be a different story.

We exchanged silver rings made from antique spoon handles, which we'd found the previous winter at a Christmas food and craft fair at Port Meirion — the model village developed by Clough Williams-Ellis in the 1920s and later used for the cult dystopian TV series, *The Prisoner*.

Inexpensive and celebratory, it felt good to have taken two and a half years to take the next fork along the path. We followed it with two weeks in Portugal, courtesy of NB, whose place we had rented in Hebden Bridge for a couple of nights when we'd had a book launch there. NB had since emigrated and offered us two weeks for £100 and, when he discovered we were on honeymoon, moved us from the tiny rental cottage to his own house on the beautiful quinta in the countryside near Fundão.

Travel became a thread of our relationship. For launches, and as much slow travel as we could inexpensively manage around Europe. Often the trips were helped by writing grants or gifts, like the momentous journey to Toledo, courtesy of A.'s dad, Ming.

I'd wanted to see the places that Casilda might have seen since I was twelve years old. The Alcázar of her day has been twice rebuilt but two sites in the city have remained unchanged. What is now the Museum of Spanish Magic, the only museum of its kind in Spain, is housed in an Islamic cave-house from the tenth century. Amongst occult texts and artefacts from a hodgepodge of faiths, is a faded wall-painting of a hand of Fatima or Hamsa, a symbol to avert evil from the original house. I doubt that Casilda, a princess of the city, ever visited this home, but it was part of her landscape. So too was a tiny mosque that later became a Catholic chapel known as Cristo de la Luz, with an apse added to the Moorish building. In Casilda's day it was Mezquita Bab-al-Mardum, named for the nearest city gate near what is now the Puerta del Sol, in what used to be the Medina.

Both cave-house and mosque entrance me, and at the mosque…

The world is white.

…water against stone. Is there a word in the breeze? Tulaytula.

Remember, my darling Casilda. Remember… and if you can't remember, invent…

Remember how you heard the story of Saint Marina, fascinated by a king's daughter who ran away to lead a contemplative's life…

…there is a rustle of silk, shadows beneath vaulted arches… water bells against stone, whispers, Casilda.

And there she is — in the tiny garden of the Mesquita Bab-al-Mardum. She opens her arms to embrace her futures, whispers her name into the breeze: Casilda. And I turn to face her, as though looking into a mirror…

But there is only a shadow, pale as dust, that flits across a mote of light, the fragrance of roses suffusing the air. Somewhere a string is plucked, faint music —

Al-ʿūdu qud tarannam

Bi-abdāʾi talhīn

Wa ŝaqqod al-mad ā nib

Riyād al-basātîn

The scent of roses… and A. calling my name…

Lughnasadh to Samhain

August 1, 2024…

Between light and loss, tawny owls call night into being, serenading the moon. Their voices are ghosts that I carry like ancestors, shadows — golden and dark — the soft sounds of dreams, memories strung across years, voices of starlight from places long gone.

Tawny owls are territorial and defend a large area, so it's likely that this is one pair. The female calls *kewick* (often heard as too-wit), the male replies *hoo-hoo*. Beautiful birds with fluffy round faces, large round eyes. The longest recorded age is over twenty-three years but many live for only four years and a large percentage don't make it to breeding age (one year). It's our fourth winter here and I'm hoping ours will make it through another year, and another…

Their calls are enthusiastic during the full moon and I cheer their hunts as they call deliriously into the night. My son, S, contracted Lyme disease in our first summer in the forest, eating into years of his life. In Finistère Lyme has increased enormously, largely because fox hunting has almost entirely wiped out the local fox population. An adult fox can eat over 5,000 mice a year, and mice are the biggest vector for Lyme-bearing ticks. With the demise of foxes the mouse population has exploded, particularly in mast years when beech or oak trees bear bumper crops of nuts or acorns, adding a rich food supply to swell their unchecked population.

Ironically, the farmers, who are often the keenest hunters, end up buying expensive and toxic chemicals to defend their crops from the out-of-control mouse population. Taking apex hunters out of an ecosystem is a disaster for plants, non-human animals, humans… A pair of owls eat many fewer mice than one fox, even when they have a brood to feed. But they are doing their part, along with a pair of buzzards who enjoy posing as statues and calling like cats.

Making a home in the forest is a long process of renovation. In the first months here, A. and I camped in a room that my son has now colonised as an exercise space, living out of suitcases while a bedroom was built into the attic. The *grenier* room covers the whole top floor, has art and music spaces for A. and a corner where I have an occasional desk. When it was ready, we painted the wooden floors blue-grey and laid old rugs in warm autumn oranges and reds from sellers in Morocco. I bought another for my writing room that turned out to be infested with moth larvae. I tried essential oils, a natural insecticide, then anything I could get my hands on — keeping the rug out on the deck. The moths kept coming and finally we sealed the squirming rug in a plastic box, heavily doused, and left it away from the house.

Between the enchantment of the owl and the battle with carpet moths, the first leaks in the roof appeared, though it would take another two years to discover that the tiles were disintegrating — slates turning to mud. Mudstone to slate… the story of Blodeuwedd, the life in North Wales… slate back to mud… a new life in a forest in France…

Will we be flowers or owls?

What are you doing here, Jan?

Wonder and struggle.

And that soul-tingling call — *kewick — hoo-hoo kewick — hoo-hoo.*

How a break can become a turning point. The rib is slowly healing. For months it has whispered about the need to change, to slow… And then my ankle swells — just the right ankle, a bruise of burst capillaries blooming blue-purple, a persistent ache. The little toe numb, the foot cold.

I have yearned for summer through a wet May, grey June, damp early July. Blue sky, expansiveness, desire bursting into heat, humidity treacle thick, 33 degrees in our (as yet uninsulated) attic bedroom at night, but the right foot remains cold. And — the desire fulfilled — I find myself nettled, prickly, unsettled, not wanting heat, but yearning for autumn…

In spring I made nettle soup, a nettle iron tonic, nettle cake from the strained leftovers. Now, in August, I gather seeds from the garden's abundance of nettles. Full of linoleic and linolenic acids, vital for making omega 3 and omega 6. They have crunch and a slight saltiness, are rich in iron and vitamin C. Tiny powerhouses that work on the adrenals, tonic for fatigue. But stimulating — not for sticky evenings when I crave sleep.

Exhaustion builds, nimbus clouds waiting to storm. A herbalist mentor helps me navigate remedies for an assortment of maladies, none of them terrible, but there is a pattern that I know I am missing… I massage my ankle with horse chestnut and wintergreen, put comfrey on the rib, push myself to keep working so that I can take a sabbatical in the autumn…

This cusp of August — heat then rain, the briefest of summers, a month with nettle. It's a plant (and food) with one of the widest ranges of benefits for a plethora of conditions and constitutions. A plant we learn to recognise early in life, in tandem with dock or plantain, reaching for leaves to soothe nettle's stings.

I think I know her, this herb that every child is wary of. How difficult it can be to see those we think we know by heart. All the facts are in my head — leaves that astringe the gut, clear congestion, catarrh, bronchitis, coughs… that are strong antihistamines. Nettle has an affinity with the kidneys, helping to clean the blood. She's a diuretic, relieving fluid retention, helpful with cystitis, aiding the excretion of uric acid, so beneficial for gout and arthritis. Nettle modulates inflammation, soothes peptic ulcers and acid reflux, cools acne, eczema, urticaria, and psoriasis, calms diarrhoea and gastritis. An excellent tonic for anaemia, an immune-boost after illness, her juice treats wounds, haemorrhoids, burns, staunches bleeding… Nettle has strong associations with the female reproductive system, regulating periods and stimulating lactation. For all her fieriness and sharp boundaries, she is a generous soul.

In this sticky month of harvests I pull cards for a writing circle I've gathered — two images — one of them of a frog. I read about the frog's incredibly sensitive skin and I'm a child again — too 'thin-skinned', too 'sensitive'. Later, I sit with nettle — the seed tincture, warming and earthy, moves to my heart, opens a space to listen to my sensitive skin, a space for boundaries — she has her sting for all her generosity.

Nettle is a herb of Mars. Once, I was adept at righteous indignation — political activism, feminist causes. Now injustice and inequity evoke more sorrow than fury. There is so much violence done in our names — drones chasing children, people enslaved to supply what we consume daily... How do we live in a world that breaks our hearts and go on creating? How do we witness to the suffering of the world without hardening our sensitive skins?

A time to sting and a time to nourish, nettle sings. She is all fire, and yet, internally, nettle cools — cleansing the blood, soothing the adrenals, lowering stress, bringing peace where allergies and inflammation flare hot.

Make peace with living in a sensitive skin, nettle whispers, as she nettles me not to fear fire and heat.

Walking in the forest that surrounds the house, a gathering of plants and butterflies, trees and birds, insects and animals. I stop again and again — a world on fire, a world of abundance —

honeysuckle

valerian

nettle

cow wheat

royal fern

bramble

gallic rose

pennywort

enchanter's nightshade

bittercress

bird's foot trefoil

meadowsweet

marsh thistle

yellow pimpernel

campion

loosestrife

sweet briar

Last year, on a tiny patch of scrubby ground at the entrance to the forest, a little enclave of flowers appeared overnight. A profusion of borage, meadowsweet, and magically, one tall yellow evening primrose. After the October storms, the patch was devastated by heavy machinery that went in to extract fallen trees. I thought there would be no growth this year, the ground churned and compacted. But late in the summer a single evening primrose springs up… then more and more. A vulnerable-looking flower rising from a small patch of traumatised ground.

At the end of August my youngest 'child' turns thirty. It's a quiet day — S has been ill for three and a half years.

A few days later A. and I are on the ferry for a month in the UK — meetings, a book launch, visits to family and friends, a few days at the end to gather ourselves in a friend's tiny barn conversion in Cornwall that we return to at the end of each visit.

Betony travels with me through a September.

Wood betony (*Betonica officinalis*) is part of the mint family. In Spain there is the saying, *He has as many virtues as betony.* In Italy the maxim is, *Sell your coat and buy betony.* And the American herbalist John Sauer says, *There is no illness brought by cold in which betony cannot be administered effectively.* In Gaelic, wood betony is simply called lus bheathag, or 'Life Plant'.

betonica officinalis

wood betony

common hedge-nettle

purple betony

bishop's wort

canadian lousewort

heal all

lus bheathag

Slightly warming, drying, aromatic, betony can also be cooling for lung conditions. He is a nervine tonic, an ally for stress and a muscle relaxant who helps to clear the mind and dispel brain fog. He strengthens digestive processes and stimulates digestive juices. But perhaps his most vital characteristic is how grounding betony is. Away with the faeries, too much in my head, liable to forget my body… betony is a friend.

The Anglo Saxon Herbal recommends an infusion to prevent:

frightful nocturnal goblins and terrible sights and dreams.

In Wales betony charms were protection against bad dreams, and growing betony around the house would guard the inhabitants from 'all mischeefes'.

It's been many years since I was last in Bristol. We have a meal with young friends — LM, who I've known since he was 4, who used to devise wild adventures with my youngest daughter while the older children hung back, askance, and his partner, B. On our eighth anniversary, A. and I share small plates sitting on a covered balcony on the dock after seeing Constable's 'Hay Wain' at an exhibition at the Bristol Museum and Art Gallery. We were captivated too by a Ben Rivers film about an old guy living in a wilderness hut in Scotland, who talked about how the earth had waited for humanity to evolve in order to have an audience. I'm not sure I'm convinced, but recognise the longing to be seen…

Thirty years ago I was ordained in Bristol Cathedral — March 12, 1994. A stone plaque was installed to commemorate this historic event. The first women ordained priests in the Church of England were invited to pay for it. And on it were none of their names — only the names of the three men who led the service — the Right Reverend Barry Rogerson, together with the precentor, John Simpson, and the Dean of the Cathedral, Wesley Carr. After twenty-eight years of pressure, a new plaque was installed, carved in Welsh slate and bearing the names of the thirty-two women — nine have died, several others, like me, have left ministry. The media reports of how the women ordained in 1994 gathered to watch the unveiling were something of an exaggeration.

I have not entered the cathedral since the day of the ordination — thirty years and six months. Stepping inside feels momentous. A. and I search for the plaque, search again and finally ask the person on the entrance desk where to find it. She is uncertain but thinks it may be somewhere near the front on the left. A. finally locates a glimpse of it — a barrier taller than me stands around the area, behind it piles of metal boxes full of sound, lighting and film equipment. A. worms through the cables and around the barrier with my phone but can't get close enough to capture an image. As he makes the attempt my temperature drops. I stand shivering like someone in shock.

Why do I need to see my name on the wall of a place I have no faith in?

What are you doing here?

I need to be outside, away… back to the art gallery, to Richard Long's slate installation — a circle of thick blocks and slabs of slate in rusts and greens and every shade of grey, reminding me of North Wales… back to the little garden cottage where we were staying, to be among

jasmine

honeysuckle

crane's bill

The next morning I buy a spray of flowers from a tiny florist in Clifton

sunflowers

common burnet

corymb flower tansy

alpine delphinium

wild mint

love in a mist

star scabious

astrantia

We move on to visit my daughter, T, and her family, walk in woods with grandchildren, visit Kenilworth Castle, a place where we used to spend time with other home-educating friends when we lived in Birmingham. One family moved to Norfolk, another to mid-Wales. LM, who we had dinner with in Bristol, is their youngest son. We'll see JM, their older son, in a few days along with their parents, dearest of friends, V and CM, recently diagnosed with motor neurone disease.

We leave for London the next day and I wake early, covered in angry patches of red skin — bites, I think at first, but no… they persist for the rest of the trip, fragments of hot, dry inflammation coming and going. Soon, joints swell, redden, ache, and my ankle remains bloated and painful. I have no vocabulary for the tiredness, which pulls me back to the decade of fatigue after the assaults.

But it is a joy to see family and friends. In London we meet my oldest daughter, R, at Tate Modern. A superb Blaue Reiter exhibition. The Zenele Muholi exhibition, focussing on hate crimes against the black LGBTQIA+ community in South Africa, is unsettling, difficult and courageous. My trans daughter has visited it several times.

Whenever I visit an art exhibition there is a point when overwhelm hits me, forcing me to pause and let trance calm me. At Tate Modern I generally head for the room of Gerhard Richter abstracts that remind me of lakes. I sit and fall into them. But today I discover a room of Joan Mitchell nature abstracts, fall in love, return the next day to sit with 'Two Sunflowers', losing all sense of time, absorbed in vibrant yellows, quieting greens, flashes of mauve, sapphire, brown… I've always associated sunflowers with my son, S, — their energy, a distinctive light…

We meet R again to visit bookshops — the treat of English-language bookshops — all year I have been hungry for story. I won't see R again for at least another eight months and fear for her safety in this brittle, fast and sometimes hostile city… but today we delight in her company.

We are due to return to spend two more nights with T and pick up the car, but she rings to say they have an infection — it might be nothing, but we do not want to risk taking a bug to V and CM in mid-Wales. Instead we drive to a tiny lodge near Tintern. It's decorated to appeal to race-goers at Chepstow — no oven, two electric rings, two pans — both for frying, a mock Louis XIV bed, painted silver with a scarlet headboard.

A. has never been to the Forest of Dean and the abbey is a place of memory for me. On a warm autumn day A. sketches while I journal about my growing list of symptoms. I've been talking to herbalists and to my doctor, thinking about how to slow down, puzzling over a pattern that I'm still not quite seeing.

It's good to go on to Ceredigion, with V and CM. V cooks roast veg with feta and bulgur wheat, leek and potato soup. We toast friendship. CM's diagnosis is heart-breaking. How can the universe be so wrong? The same universe that has a human species bent on destroying our only home while committing genocide. The same universe that has forests and lakes, sunflowers and my amazing grandchildren…

We have lunch at the pink café, now a bustling haven of inventive lunches, where once V and I took our children to be greeted by a grumpy owner who sold us the last piece of stale cake and then, when the people behind us in the queue complained there was nothing left, cut the cake we'd bought in half and sold it again. Now this corner of Ceredigion bursts with craft and gastronomy — the next day we feast on home-made pasta and foraged Welsh seafood in a community pub, celebrating JM and the team he's been working with, who return triumphant from winning the UK street food championships.

It's hard to say another goodbye and unsettling to be heading north. A. and I have agreed we won't stop at Tanygrisiau. Four years feels too soon to visit this place that we left, and love still. This place where I found sanctuary for almost twenty years. We pass it in the car and I shoot a small video as we make for an overnight stay at an inn near Betws-y-Coed. Late in the evening R calls, distressed… her marriage unravelling, life imploding. Ragged after a sleepless night, we move to a friend's cottage the next morning, and I manage to teach a herb course online that evening.

The next day is our first in-person launch since Covid. The last launch I did was for *Writing Down Deep* — my book on creative writing. We launched it in Greenwich library, R interviewing me between readings. The room was full, including the friend who'd presided at our wedding, AC, who I'd known since Rotherhithe days, and another I'd been at theological college with — an American priest in London, AK. February 2020. The last days of what now feels like a former world.

At Jo's excellent café in Bangor I read from my new novel, *smiling at grief in a house in a forest where life grows*, alongside two poets. The place is packed. There are people for each of us and for me — neighbours from Tanygrisiau, a Cinnamon author visiting from

Germany… An extraordinary evening.

We drive to Hay-on-Wye, stopping at Rhayader to visit a friend's art studio, carrying away an owl in Indian ink. It's Autumn Equinox — Alban Elfed, Light of the Water in the Druid tradition. The second of the harvest festivals, day and night in brief equilibrium before the nights grow longer and winter returns.

What have I gathered this year?

In Hay I catch up on work between forays to bookshops, which seem the most magical, luxurious buildings in the UK. We linger in the Poetry Bookshop, chatting with the wonderful owner, CP, and arranging an event for Cinnamon's twentieth anniversary next year.

Boscastle — last of eleven stops in a month.

I love this barn — its striped blue pottery, CB's welcoming pea soup and homemade bread, the attic bedroom and view across the Atlantic across wild fields. I'm ready for home, ready to turn inwards towards winter. *Create,* betony hums when I relax into the rhythm of his breath in the little cottage. We listen to wind howling grief, to rain lashing land and sea, to a weeping sky so fierce it rattles our bones. Omar sends poems from Beirut under siege, where he lives with his wife and small daughter, his extended family. How can the elements do anything but rage and keen?

I dream of my Nanna F's house, of friends and family packed into its many rooms, in danger, waiting for me to do something… do something… while another friend sets the place on fire and the extinguishers are empty and I can't find water… Wake to a heart-rending conversation with R, another with my youngest daughter who has been ill and is so far away, teaching in Korea, but she's bought paints, is making art as well as teaching, doing an MA, quilting…

Antonius Musa, a physician to Emperor Caesar Augustus, recorded forty-seven ways to use wood betony. So many virtues. I'd hoped betony might keep me from feeling fragmented and ungrounded as we moved from place to place. Souls don't travel as fast as cars and trains. In the Druid herbal system, betony is a herb of the season from Lughnasadh to the Autumn Equinox, protective of body and emotions; strengthening the solar plexus, the place from which we feel connected. The incarnative herb. He has been all of that in this nomadic month. But I long for home — to see S, and our vociferous, neurotic cat, Freyja, to soak in the bath, eat scrambled eggs, sleep in our own bed…

On the ferry home, I take drops of betony and feel drowsy, soothed.

Back home, the year turns to October and a month with Angelica.

June 2019, before Covid was a word on our lips, A. and I spent a charmed couple of weeks with a beloved friend, IL, in the Var, a wonderful place in the Provence-Alpes-Côte d'Azur region, surrounded by mountains with views all the way to the sea and the Italian Alps. One hot bright day we drove through forests that mantled the slopes of the Alpes-Maritime to meet a gifted herbalist. OS invited us to walk in her garden. Between the herbs and bushes, large jars of oils macerated in the sun, the essence of plants being drawn into viscous liquid. As we wandered OS conversed a little, listened, stopped by a patch of frondy angelica, sunny with tiny yellow flowers that would give way to vivid green pom-poms of seeds, and asked A. if digestion was something that concerned him.

Yes.

And anxiety?

Yes.

This is your plant.

Warming, soothing angelica.

How are you digesting your life? she asked.

This autumn, my digestion is off — it has burnt hard and hot, only to become stagnant and cold. I'm craving chilli and ginger, rosemary and angelica. I'm on sabbatical but struggling to do the creative work I'd imagined having time for, can't recall how I've so recently managed to work long hours, but now feel days slipping away unused. Time slippery as mist.

Angelica relaxes body tissues and emotions, warms, travels to the lungs, clears and deepens breath. Her ability to help blood flow to the brain is part of what makes her a strong nerve tonic.

clarity

digestion

warmth

Inspiration on the warm breath of autumn. I breathe in angelica oil, the steam of angelica tea. I have no skill in drawing, but take a double spread of my journal, find coloured pencils, draw a field — a clearing amongst woodland. Autumn is a time of beginnings, the seed time. I draw the things I'm harvesting as dandelion heads fat with seed, draw airy angelica as my work in progress. Elderberries and rosehips for work completed — a novel, courses taught. Bulbs — iris versicolor and sweet flag — for the future.

On sabbatical, I'm walking more, but noticing it in my knees and the inflamed ankle. I diffuse angelica oil, dilute it to add to baths for muscles and joints.

Before walking in the forest I place drops of angelica root tincture on my tongue — viscous and warm, a burst of aromatic spice, copper and green, a hint of bitter and, as I set off along the forest path, a surge of radiance. Lightness fills my head, settles behind my eyes, eases my breath. The taste on my tongue, sticky and autumn-warm. I walk listening to blackbirds, who will stay all winter. Along the track, two-year-old stems of angelica — hollow, the colour of soft cardamon, some as tall as me, their umbels skeletal, some with seeds still clinging like tiny brown-paper packages.

I'm preparing for my final exam as a herbal practitioner. What we might mean by healing has been a thread for so long — in ministry, as an editor midwifing books into the world, as a writer weaving stories. With the herbs I offer to accompany others as a bridge between plants and those asking what healing might look like when it's not defined as 'cure', but negotiation with and adaptation to real bodies.

At night I listen to the owls, watch the moon wax and wane, anxious for family and friends, slowly digesting the answer to the puzzle of symptoms that has built all year. Skin flares and inflamed joints, dry eyes and throat, the broken rib that was never broken at all, but was costochondritis, an inflammation of the cartilage connecting the ribs to the breastbone, the vascular issues and swelling of my ankle… After a year of chasing symptoms I have an answer.

What will this autoimmune condition mean?

Since the assaults I've lived with fluctuating energy, fitting the voluntary passions of Cinnamon Press and writing around troughs of fatigue, periductal mastitis and leftover injuries. The new diagnosis feels like going back decades, especially when more than one health practitioner suggests it's likely the assaults were the origin of what I am learning to adapt to now.

Angelica root was once hung over doors to ward off darkness, over beds to fend off nightmares. Each day angelica is with me — *tend to heart, to gut, rekindle the flame.*

She is the herb of angels, of winter stories of the birth of a golden child who brings light. In the Druid tradition, Alban Arthan — the Light of Winter — is the return of a divine child, the Mabon. Rebirth of the golden Solstice sun, the return of warmth, light, life. Light in the darkness. We are two months away from the shortest day, the longest night. I sense the dark, but am held by angelica's warmth and light.

First comes Samhain. Another year cycled. The veil between worlds gossamer, the darkness deep, new moon dark before waxing again, rumblings of horror across the world.

What are you doing here?

For the joy of the sweet green earth

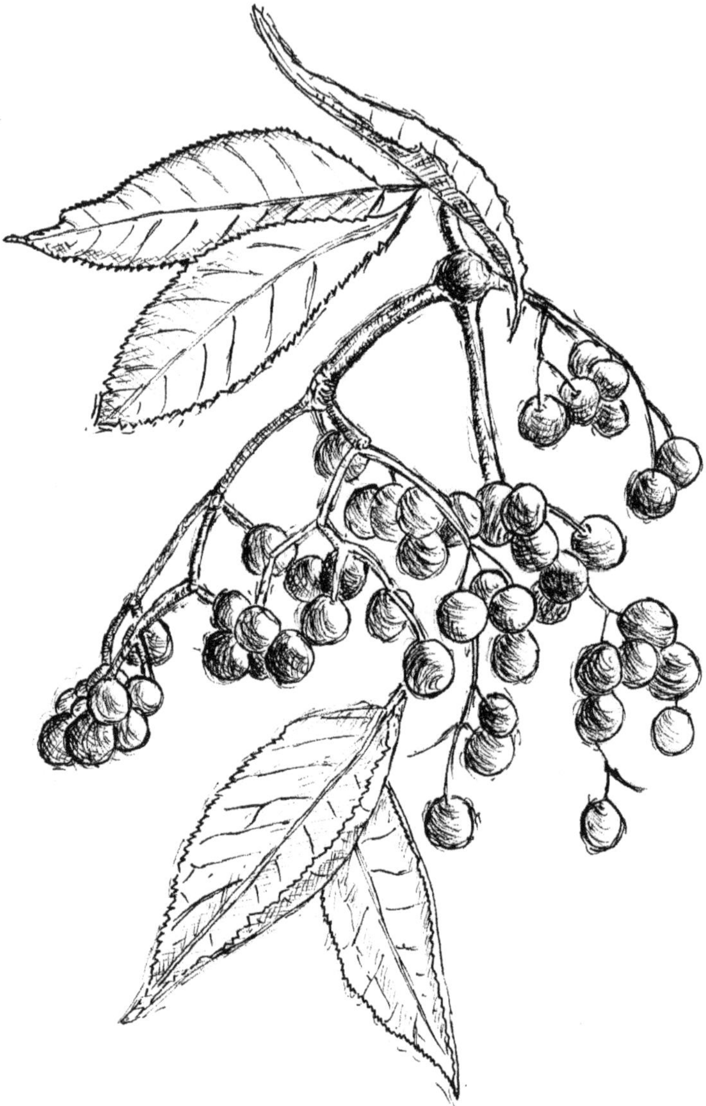

In the dark wood

Ursula Le Guin tells us that forest is the word for the world. In 2020 the forest grew dark for all of us. And through it all, the voice of the sweet green earth, singing streams, keening waves, crescendoing mountains, chanting woodlands, persisted.

Before the pandemic, A. and I had begun searching for a home in a forest. It started with travelling to write — the thought experiments of 'what if we lived here' that we imagined we would never act on. But wondering coalesced into something stronger and more insistent after the shock of the Brexit vote with its savage shadow of isolationism. At the same time, my herbal studies whispered of forest, a space to change pace and practice as I moved towards whatever elderhood might bring.

What are you doing here?

Becoming a different story. Becoming a herbalist in a forest where I'll find the next fork along the path.

When my children were small I'd turn to herbs and essential oils as home-remedies and had long dreamed of studying herbalism. A. not only encouraged me to let that dream breathe, but used his savings to make it so. The path began in a wonderful school offering an aromatherapy diploma. In 2019, travelling from Turin to visit IL in the Var, when I'd met the gifted herbalist, OS. Inspired, I searched out a herbal apprenticeship — a mix of intense weekends and self-directed work with a stress on hands-on, highly sensory learning. The first two weekends were magical.

Then, in autumn 2019, we visited Huelgoat, where the forest felt like home. We returned to Wales determined to move.

There are so many ways to unsettle.

It took five months to get the process started. I needed a lawyer to persuade M to sign the papers that had been stipulated in the divorce settlement, the estate agents were chaotic, and my over-thinking mind began to second-guess heart and gut — was leaving a pretence? Did I actually want this?

My body couldn't believe I might leave this beloved house in Wales.

My body yearned for the forest in Finistère.

In February 2020 my youngest daughter, C, made it home from China, where she had been teaching. In the picture she sent from the plane before taking off she looked so young and alone in her black face mask. She had already had Covid, though we hadn't known the name for it then.

Her older sister, T, had just let me know she was pregnant with her second child.

A. and I visited his dad, Ming, and A. stayed with him while I travelled to London to launch my creative writing book, *Writing Down Deep*. It had been three years in the making and the launch, in the beautiful domed library in Greenwich, surrounded by friends, family and kind strangers, compèred by R, my oldest daughter, was extraordinary. We had no idea it would be Cinnamon Press's last live launch until September 2024. We didn't imagine that it would be the last time A. and I would see Ming.

We thought that soon we would set out to search for a home in the forest, not imagining the seriousness of the pandemic hurtling towards us, but by the end of February collective anxiety was rising. R emailed that she could no longer get the vitamin D pills she relied on to help with MS — it was one of the things people were already panic-buying. We showed our first potential buyers around the house with face masks on and without shaking hands. Launch venues and literary festivals cancelled events just as a group of writers arrived for an intense few days of writing workshops in our home and JM arrived to cater for the course and deliver a workshop on writing from taste.

We had many conversations about what a 'safe space' might mean that week, some of them heated. One of our number left during the first night, a good friend and excellent poet who needed the security of home. IL had to leave before the end of the course when President Macron gave French people a tight deadline to get home or be locked out of the country. And yet we wrote to the end of our hearts.

A. and I delivered workshops, JM's taste session was loved and my son, S, produced a superb session on writing from our immediate contexts — none of us realising how prophetic his workshop might be. We shared JM's sourdough focaccia, polenta with reblochon cheese, slow-cooked tomato ragù with root vegetable, hazelnut and mushroom sausages, meltingly rich crostata di marmellata, drank earthy coffee and endless herbal teas for the respiratory system, while I diffused antimicrobial essential oils in every room. On the last night, my daughter, C, cooked an astonishing feast and we decorated the kitchen with greenery, golden gorse flowers and candles.

No one got sick. Everyone got home safely, though JM was caught by the lockdown and stayed on with us for another ten weeks of that strangest of times. The herbal apprenticeship was put on hold (and wouldn't be completed until summer 2022, online, from the forest in Finistère, with only two of the twenty original students left). With bookshops and the Welsh distribution centre closed (while other distribution ground to a halt more slowly) I was consumed with saving Cinnamon Press from extinction.

There would be no more people viewing our house.

> Give sorrow words, the grief that does not speak knits up the o'er wrought heart and bids it break.
>
> *Macbeth, Act 4, Sc.3*

Death counts rose slowly, inexorably, the lockdown elongated, announced with increasingly hollow political rhetoric. I wrote an online course on hope and creativity — 40 Degrees of Connection — with short audio segments for each day. We did a family Zoom (a new phenomenon for us) with T on her birthday. She still had Hyperemesis gravidarum, the extreme form of morning sickness that had plagued her first pregnancy, but she was more relaxed with F home (furloughed from work) and grateful for the joy of their garden. On screen, I noticed R was beardless and looked much younger.

Good Friday: 10 April. Day 19 of Lockdown:

> A day off that feels like paradise in the midst of apocalypse. We would love this at another time — no planes, less pollution, sunshine, time to make shower gel, to linger over a dinner of risotto and C's Victoria sponge, just baked, watch episodes of *Mushishi,* an exquisitely drawn Japanese anime set in an imaginary past that suggests panpsychism…, talk about art, spend hours writing. So blessed. So fragile. But I don't know when I will next see T and her family, or R. 980 people died of Covid today in the UK. Bangor University is being converted into a temporary hospital. An image of mass burials in New York, workers in hazmat suits as plain wooden coffins are stacked in a trench. An apocalypse with a slick veneer for those not on the front line.

We booked to travel on the first ferry sailing to Finistère at the end of June. Lockdown remained tighter in Wales than England so we took the fastest route to the border, breathless to make it to Brittany, where we viewed houses in a daze — more than I can remember. One, with caged dogs crying in the garden and a picture on the wall of the entrance hall, mother and daughter pointing hunting rifles at one another. One with a tiny patch of forest beyond its rambling garden and beautiful, neglected spaces, backing onto a battery-chicken farm. The house we most wanted to view was withdrawn from sale and, panicked, we settled on another — a long low building, smaller than we'd imagined, and outside the forest, but with a stone barn that might one day be a writing and herbal centre.

Only one couple had viewed Meirion House before lockdown, but

I phoned them and they put in an offer the next day while we signed a *compromis de vente*, on the long house near Carnoët. But the forest had not given up on us. The evening before we were due to sail home, we noticed the house we had wanted to view had its 'for sale' sign displayed again. There was no answer when we phoned so we drove back and found the owner in the garden, feeding sheep and goats in his animal sanctuary. We viewed the house early the next morning and everything in us said yes. The contract was organised over the phone in a supermarket car park and I signed it (digitally) onboard the ferry, minutes before sailing shut us off from the signal.

Gut and heart made the decisions — the serendipity of seeing the sale notice, being the first viewers, a sliver of timing.

We had no chain in the UK and our buyers weren't dependent on selling their home, making this the simplest of conveyances. But nothing went smoothly. Our buyers' lawyer dropped out, the estate agents could not have been less interested, contracts stalled and complications appeared daily. But I had dropped into the consciousness of the child exhilarated by red and cobalt shimmers on stone from sun on stained glass, who could lose time by a stream in Kirkleatham woods. We were going to the forest.

And so we packed and cleared twenty years of family life. In mid-September A. and S left for a short-term rental in Brittany to establish residency, while C and I continued to pack and clean. Each day I fielded fraught emails and phone calls about the sale process with a quiet certainty that this move would happen.

At Autumn Equinox T gave birth to IE, a daughter born at home — the home-birth a gift from K, my friend from Cephas and bridesmaid at both my weddings. During Covid home-birth services had shut down and fathers were banished from being present at the hospital. K paid for a private midwife. The home-birth was a healing for T and F, after the trauma of T's first birth experience in hospital, and meant that their three-year-old son, MTF, was there at the moment his sister entered the world — he remembers it still. I would meet the small miracle of IE online two days later.

Before the end of that week, two-thirds of Wales had returned to lockdown. By early October the lawyer handling the conveyancing stopped responding to emails. The sellers in the forest lost hope that we would ever move.

There was so much to let go — toys and clothes from the childhoods of four children, more books than we could carry with us, the house I loved, love still. I'd spent a third of my life, almost half of my adult life in that house — there I home-educated four children, sought sanctuary after assaults, divorced and married, founded Cinnamon Press, celebrated birthdays and festivals, hosted meals for family, neighbours, authors, taught writing courses, read books to my children, wrote books, cried rivers, laughed and danced.

The weeks of packing done, I spent a day moving from room to room, soaking up the memories of each one, woke the next morning hollow and desolate, knowing that everything in my life was about to become unfamiliar — language, house, culture, how we would run Cinnamon Press, how I would even make the journey to France in such strange times, lockdown closing in around me… And yet there was so much to move toward.

We had still not exchanged contracts when the removers arrived the next day, but our buyers were adamant it would happen — a day, maybe two… and if I sent the removers away I'd lose the fees we'd paid, with no idea of when we might next be able to move — a blanket lockdown was looming.

C and I ate dinner with neighbours that evening and slept in a holiday cottage a few doors from our house — our beds already in the enormous van. The next morning the removers finished and I sat on the floor in an empty house, waiting for the phone call about the exchange of contracts, which didn't come.

Wandering through the rooms, I found a forgotten journal in my empty bedroom — a patchy record from a dark time…

When C was born my parents decided they would visit. It was a few months after Dad's return from the Philippines, their relationship at its most volatile. They had taken no interest in the pregnancy, my mother telling me I could 'always get rid of it' when I'd phoned to tell her I was having a third child, but there they were. I'd arranged for close friends, KP and NP, to look after R and T while I was having the C-section, but my mother overruled her grandchildren being looked after by strangers, especially one of 'them' (NP was not white). C was born late on a Friday morning in January and my parents arrived at the hospital shortly after, full of anger, R and T in tow.

As they entered the side room where I'd been taken after surgery, buried scraps of memory surfaced, overwhelming me. A nurse glanced at me, took my falling blood pressure and ushered my parents out, sadly with my distressed children. I told M to go with them, come back when he could, R and T should not be left with them. The darkness that bubbled up in the days that followed could not dim the light of that rosy, dark-eyed girl newly come into the world and we cleaved to one another.

In the first months of C's life, I spent hours sitting on the floor of the tiny third bedroom in front of an old Amstrad word processor, breastfeeding as I completed my PhD thesis, the final structure coming to me in snatches of dream. I had the viva that summer, aware that a doctorate in feminist theology would make me more vulnerable in a church that did not ordain women to the priesthood and found mothers in holy orders too bodiful, too strange, too much even without a PhD in feminist theology. During the maternity leave it was suggested that I should leave the curacy early. I was offered posts that were then withdrawn, the future becoming stark. Postpartum was a heady mix of exhaustion and elation — for my children, for my research… muddied with memories awakened when my parents had walked in after C's birth. Memories that M did not want to hear, even on the day I pushed my hand through an upstairs window.

A tiny sickle of scar at the base of my thumb and the journal I found on the last day at Tŷ Meirion were all that held this story — one that preceded another house move — to a place where the congregation had traded hope for blame, where S was born, five months after being priested. The last lines I wrote in that journal were from January 1994, a few weeks pregnant with S —

> What a place to have a child! Life in all its fullness… the darkness has not overcome it… I'm barely clinging on.

I burnt the journal page by page in the wood burner in the empty kitchen of Tŷ Meirion, locked up and returned to the cottage where C and I waited for the exchange to happen. It didn't and I returned to our long-time home the next day to say a final goodbye to each room, steeling myself to make calls and send emails — over and over.

The deposit had cleared and our buyers were as keen as me to get the lawyers to act. Between fraught emails I learnt that my Eurostar to Calais had been cancelled. I looked at flights — none. Eurostar offered a train to Lille or nothing, so I changed the booking, found a train to get me from Lille to Rennes, cancelled the hotel that A. would have used if he'd been picking me up from Calais. I made rapid decisions as though viewing my life from a distance while the world prepared to shut down again. When the last iota of travel was in place I managed to get my elusive lawyer on the phone. It was late afternoon and he told me now we had to wait for the top of the chain to complete. The total chain had only ever consisted of me and our buyer. I demanded he complete now, this moment, while I stayed on the line. He did.

The next day C and I set out for T's house, where C would stay to continue working online, teaching English to children in China. Kind neighbours drove us to Llandudno Junction, where police checked we had an essential reason to travel. The train arrived half an hour late, a ghost train with a scatter of passengers keeping their distance, bound for Milton Keynes. It terminated at Chester. The replacements would require five changes. Instead we bought new tickets for a direct train most of the way, which was also late, ensuring we would miss our final connection. Yet eventually we arrived — tired and elated — to meet IE, three and a half weeks old and beautiful. As we travelled, Boris Johnson announced he would go for a 'no deal' Brexit.

After two days with T and her family I left for London where I'd booked a tiny but beautiful hotel room, heavily discounted as lockdown approached again. I'd planned for a couple of days so I could see R and the friend who had presided at our wedding before leaving the UK, but the day before I arrived restaurants closed and R and AC couldn't travel across the city. The hotel served dinner on the first evening, then closed its kitchen. I sourced sandwiches from almost-deserted shops in St Pancras Station, eerie in its emptiness. I video-called R, desolate that we could not meet. Since February R's hair had reverted to a wild teenage mop of curls — the hipster look, with beard and trimmed hair, completely erased.

At the Eurostar gate a security guard herded passengers, screaming at those who froze in confusion, constantly shouting 'It's the Covid! It's the Covid!' as her colleagues rolled their eyes, shaking their heads. In the crush of people after months of isolation, my temperature soared and, once in the departure lounge, I headed for the toilet and sat for a long time in a stall, breathing without a mask. But the train was uneventful and I let myself sink into writing, oblivious until we arrived at Lille, a station that seemed full of beggars. To be homeless in a pandemic… There were no food kiosks, but I found water in a vending machine. A final train to Rennes — and — at last… A.

…and I remembered a day on a platform at Euston when A. and I were first together, A. emerging from the thinning crowd. How we held each other as though only the two of us existed, how the world dropped away, and all that remained was our embrace, A.'s lips on mine, our beating hearts…

But it was not like that in Rennes. We had dismantled our life and, deeply unsettled, awkwardness hung between us. It would take time to find equilibrium in a different story.

Eight days after I arrived in France, we signed the final contract for our new home with only hours before the next lockdown and moved to Ti Triskele that day. A day later and we could not have completed or moved. The furniture would not arrive for at least another week, but I sourced cheap crockery and cutlery, a couple of pans online and basic bedding. The house had beds and a small assortment of coffee tables to eat off. We moved in at Samhain and I made pumpkin soup.

Ti Triskele was full of dead flies and animal hair, the freezer stuffed with loaves of white bread. The used litter tray left in the living room hopped with fleas that took weeks to clear. The tap in the kitchen was broken, the shower in S's room disconnected, there were broken door handles and the basin in the downstairs toilet emptied onto the floor. The living room wall ran with water and a few days later the river burst its banks, forming a lake in the garden.

We learned to download attestation forms for each trip to the supermarket, where armed police stood at the doors. But we could walk for an hour each day in the forest that surrounded us. Frost on the grass, trees blazing with leaves in scarlet and mandarin.

In the following year S would contract Lyme disease, A.'s dad, Ming, would die before A. could get the vaccines needed to travel, I would have a flare of illness with symptoms from the days after the assaults two decades earlier and a breast scare. In the following year we would also uncover the extent of renovations needed on the house and, some days, French bureaucracy or running Cinnamon under an unfamiliar tax regime during a pandemic, or finding a dentist in another language, would leave us wondering what had possessed us to make such a move.

A. was steadfast, rooted oak to my airy, trancy mistletoe. But oak attracts lightning and, under pressure, burns hot and long. And mistletoe, overwhelmed, is less about expansive vision and more drawn to watery, inward emotion. Mistletoe that grows on oak is herbally the most powerful — an alchemical marriage. Oak's elements of earth and fire offering grounded presence to mistletoe's elements of air and water, dreams, imaginings and possibilities.

But uprooted, defamiliarised, finding ourselves without the words, without the cultural references, gestures, language that had forged us, without family and friends nearby, soaked in the losses of illness and bereavement, the alchemy unbalanced.

What are you doing here?

There were days, weeks, months when we had no answer. But there was the forest, always the forest.

> In the dark times
> Will there also be singing?
> Yes, there will be singing.
> About the dark times.
>
> Bertolt Brecht, *The Svendborg Poems*

Moon waxing and waning, owls singing in the dark.

Home to the forest

In the forest is a world and the world is life. I had followed my heart to its farthest edge to be in this forest, a place of darkness, a place of exquisite beauty.

There are so many ways to settle.

In our first full year here I wrote a haiku every few days, working through the micro-seasons of the year, based on a Japanese seasonal cycle of twenty-four seasons divided into seventy-two micro-seasons, adapted for Finistère's Celtic landscape. The observation was an act of settling.

In an unfamiliar land I wrote towards points of shared reference. The climate here is not dissimilar to Snowdonia, Breton and Welsh have much in common, both being Brythonic Celtic languages, and there is a shared sense of Celtic culture. I interspersed the haiku with eight lyric poems for the lunar and solar Celtic festivals — Imbolc, Spring Equinox, Beltane, Summer Solstice, Lughnasadh, Autumn Equinox, Samhain, Winter Solstice.

Paying attention built a tentative connection which began at Imbolc 2021, season of longing, first stirrings of spring:

Imbolc

Light comes slowly to Candlemas—
mare's-milk pale, ewes bleating rhythms
of Winter birth; life-scraps
of hope in ghosted sun,
scalpel leaves—snowdrop-thin—

pierce through earth, fisted
buds thawing ground
so recently wintered closed.

We shelter within—
kitchen a belly of scents,
birchwood flames,
comfort of poppyseed cake,
violet candles flickering chants—

Winter will pass
rains will be gone,
flowers will bloom,
seasons of singing
will come.

Charting a life unmoored from the familiar, but permeable to the new, the poetry became a way of grounding myself in a place that had called me, but would only slowly become a place where I could sense some belonging. Each haiku, just seventeen syllables, challenged me to see things differently, folded me in trance as I sat with this land whose Celtic ancestors were entwined with my own. In the first micro-sequence, the tree that suggested the promise of spring was a rowan.

In my first pregnancy I was certain I was carrying a girl and couldn't think of boys' names. During a difficult visit to my mother in Yorkshire, we went for a walk on Haworth Moor, the place of Emily Brontë's *Wuthering Heights,* which also inspired scenes in Charlotte Brontë's *Jane Eyre*. We walked the moor above Top Withens, a ruined farmhouse where rowans grow at unlikely angles from rocks and one lone rowan hangs above the waterfall. At university, Rowan Williams had been my Christology supervisor and sponsored my application to begin a PhD in feminist Christology. M had a friend, another Rowan, who'd been influential for him. So we decided on Rowan as the boy's name, though I remained certain I'd have a girl. And when he was born and my midwife asked if I was disappointed I replied — No, he's Rowan. Today Rowan is my daughter, Rowan-Echo, becoming her own story.

Rowan is a tree of magical folklore. Red the colour of warding off evil, bright berries for protection. Often planted beside houses or in churchyards, rowan provides wood for divining rods, for stirring milk to prevent it from curdling, and pocket charms against rheumatism.

Inflammation-modulating, digestive, antibacterial, and high in vitamins, especially C and A, rowan fends off scurvy. Their ripe berries make an astringent gargle for sore throats, a delicious jelly or perry. Berries can also be dried into a flour and, when fermented, yield a strong spirit. The Welsh used to brew ale from the berries, the secret of which is lost.

February was as wet as Wales in our first year — something that felt familiar, homely. What was new and delightful was that in a month of frosts in not-quite winter, not-fully spring, early flowers began to appear. We were enchanted by the wealth of birdlife and by two geese and a large duck who wandered the garden as a threesome, chattering constantly till dusk, when they would cross under the road via the river to our small front field to sleep. In its sameness and its difference, the land began to change me.

Subtle and slow. In our first March in Ti Triskele I listened to birds as I had not done since I was a seven-year-old in the woods near Kirkleatham church, and fell in love again with tawny owls.

Our tiny orchard of seven gnarled trees blossomed and everywhere yarrow uncurled in the grass, a plant that staunches wounds, lowers inflammation and blood pressure, calms anxiety. Yarrow appeared as I waited for scans after repeated bouts of mastitis reminiscent of the infections that had begun with the assaults decades earlier. I'd imagined coming to the forest to live more simply, but securing Cinnamon Press against the ravages of Covid knew no borders. We had added a new country, new language, a house in need of more renovation than we had realised and now I was ill. Amidst so much beauty, a predatory pike lurked in the river.

April 28-May 2

Yarrow in the grass,
silver-washed fritillary,
and the still pike hunts.

I turned sixty in our first May in Finistère. That January my youngest daughter had turned thirty and we'd imagined a shindig in our garden, but travel between France and the UK, where C was teaching online still waiting to be able to return to somewhere in Sout-east Asia, was at a standstill. I cooked a meal and we walked to gather hawthorn blossom for an evening tea, the full flower moon still bright.

Sixty. There were no great epiphanies, but I was in the right place, even in its strangeness.

May 29-June 3

Mugwort and sorrel,
stars of scarlet pimpernel,
foxgloves in heat, blaze.

I made elder champagne and a peppery bruschetta with the leaves of oxeye daisies. Sweet flag appeared in the river, a tame stream in summer. The shadow across the sun was that A.'s dad would never be going home. We could only wait for news, hope that he would live long enough for A. to get his next Covid vaccine and be allowed to travel to say goodbye. But Summer Solstice was bittersweet.

Midsummer

for Ming

All day it rains. In the long grass,
only the oxeye daisies
open their eyes,
elder holds armfuls of blossom—foam
to bathe the wound of her peeled-away branch—

unashamed of her body's scars and age.
The forest leans in.
Though we see no sun this longest day,
we keep a vigil far into
the shortest night, long past

the bluest hour,
wake to light subdued by clouds,
grey humidity, elder bubbling
in sugared bowls,
champagne to wish you peace at the last—
in the joy
of the sweet green earth,
in the green space of the heart,
you rest.

In the month that followed, the weather veered from rain to heat, always humid. As I taught an online course for a group of poets, a giant peacock moth flew into the room — *Saturnia pyri* — the largest European moth. A mysterious-looking creature, symbol of the unconscious and transformation. At Saint-Paul Asylum in Saint-

Remy, Provence, Van Gogh had painted her image. She returned the next day at the same time.

July 21-26

She comes in day's heat—
Saturnia pyri, wings
beating between worlds.

Some days I wondered what we had done, moving so far from those we loved, from familiarity, from a house we understood to one still unmasking its many needs. Yet always the forest called. The elder by our gate with a terrible wound, inflicted when work was done on the electric cables, healed and blossomed. Yarrow and heather flowered. The apple trees, elderly and marvellously shaped, began to fruit.

Nearing our first anniversary in the forest, while A. was away clearing his dad's house, S and I walked in the forest daily, enchanted by a huge larch near the *potterie* at the mill — a blaze of gold, protector against evil, loved by squirrels, birds, butterflies and moths:

case-bearer moth

larch pug

larch tortrix moth

Larch is an unusual conifer — he has cones like pine trees, but is deciduous, giving him added resilience in the winter. In his finery, flame-yellow and sturdy, his wood adapted to withstand even fire, he readied for another Samhain, another winter.

Each day the landscape a fraction more stripped down, the days shorter, the blaze of colours on trees dimming to mulching foliage along the paths, the river wilder. Each day the palette softening until only ivy berries blossomed — last source of nourishment for the birds each year. I walked the hollow-way in low, liquid sun, breathing in the bones of old oaks, birch, ash and elder, alders and blackthorn… I listened to the night, entranced by tawny owls, by the moon through the sloping attic window.

In December I gathered holly and ivy to make wreaths to set round candles. In parish ministry, December had been a whirlwind of Advent and Christmas activity. In the forest I nestled into softer rituals, held in the quiet of short, hushed days —

candles

comfort food

greenery

December 20-24

In winter's hedgerow,
dock, nettle, a single stand
of broom—yellow light.

The promise of Winter Solstice… knowing the light would return…

New Year brought flood from the River Squiriou. In the first year, the sudden lake in garden had been a shock, especially as we'd been assured that the flood plain was a tiny margin, not whole fields encroaching nearer and nearer the house. Now we know the rhythms, we are more sanguine, but in that first year flood water flowed with grief. Yet still owls sang into the night, sky so clear and open.

There are so many ways to settle.

Mother bear of the herbs

After my first herbal apprenticeship, disrupted by Covid, the group unravelled as we waited for in-person gatherings to begin again. In the end, when the tutors eventually agreed to finish the course online, only two of us remained to complete it. I craved more and discovered a school in Ireland that allowed me to join the second year of their apprenticeship — a mix of monthly online workshops and a curriculum that stressed contact with the herbs, culminating in an intensive week in Gorey from which I emerged as a community herbalist, just turned sixty.

I had thought this would be the end of the journey in terms of courses. But in the last months of the apprenticeship a sequence of insistent dreams unfolded. Thirty-four dreams, some bizarre and disquieting, others beautiful and compelling.

Dreams have always nudged me towards the next turn in the path — I'd dreamt the restructuring of my PhD thesis during maternity leave when I was thirty. I'd dreamt characters and events in novels, the right word for a poem, solutions to logistical problems. I've had several recurring dreams since childhood —

My Nanna's house with many more rooms than the real house — a place of endless refuge.

An anxious mothering dream of arriving at Christmas unprepared.

A dream from my days in ministry in which I'm about to take a funeral, but realise I know nothing about the family, not even the name of the loved one we are laying to rest.

A dream from childhood, that recurred from the ages of four to seven, in the house in Middlesbrough: myself, a bear called Goldie, and my imaginary friend, Marina, who could breathe underwater, being hunted by an alligator, who wears my knitted green skirt, and a stereotypical witch, gnarled, dressed in black, terrible. We run through the house, throwing our weight against a door to prevent our pursuers entering, but the door bursts open and we run to the next. The last door shuts off the kitchen from the living room. Beyond this, there is only the wild, dark night outside. And they burst through, but not to terrorise or maul us — they want only to belong. An alligator, ancient and peaceful, a crone misunderstood, whose name is Rose.

The new dreams were episodic, the same group of animals reappearing — fox, hind, cat, owl. The same plants — rose, elder, rowan, iris, hawthorn, yarrow, violet, mugwort, lavender.

In many, a wise child told me to play. In others a beautiful woman walked with me, wearing an exquisite kantha of oranges and reds, the same robe my youngest daughter had given me for my last birthday in Wales. Older, confident, a golden shadow accompanying me in my seventh decade — herbalist and story-teller. Sometimes she morphed into LC, my school headteacher, her one gold tooth gleaming as she smiled, telling me, *you are enough.*

And finally a dream of a mother bear. Wild and generous, she knew when to hibernate, when to wake, what herbs to reach for, how to protect herself. Waking after a long winter, she eased into movement, searched for herbs to heal, to stimulate gut and liver after the long sleep, becoming supple.

What are you doing here?

I woke reminded that I'd come to the forest for a different story, to live in a place where I could forage herbs, learn my craft. I would continue on after the apprenticeship, become a herbal practitioner. Go to the heart's farthest edge.

A holy thing

> It is a holy thing to love what death can touch.
>
> Anonymous

When C was born by C-section, it was the anaesthetist's first time overseeing the procedure, supervised by a consultant. My blood pressure has always been low and at a critical point I mumbled that I was going to be sick, that…

My blood pressure had dropped dangerously low and the consultant indicated this was the point the young anaesthetist should inject… some drug, the name of which vanished as consciousness swam from me. He replied he'd just go and fetch some and, even in the blur of semi-consciousness, I registered the flicker of shock and anger on the consultant's face before she hissed that he should do so at speed. It was the first time I thought I might be about to die.

I will die. But not then, nor when I was held at knife-point by a drug addict in a cold church. Not from the illnesses that consumed the years after the assaults, nor in our first year in France when my GP was so concerned by a recurrence of extreme mastitis, that I began to wonder if he was right to think the pain and swelling, itching and tenderness that resisted treatment was something sinister. The scan was a few days before my sixtieth birthday and the consultant, who had no English, repeatedly asked if I understood that it was all okay. I left clutching images of my breasts, ducts collapsed, a mass of calcifications, but no tumour. I'd felt mortality open up before me, exacerbated by being far from friends, by the knowledge that A.'s dad was dying, that our emotional tension had stretched thin as we waited for news.

Two years later my left breast once again throbbed with pain, the nipple sank and inverted. The locum doctor told me not to worry, she would just phone a few clinics to see if they could fit me in *now* (on a Friday evening). She got no response, but promised an appointment first thing Monday morning. Nothing to worry about...

Another false alarm. More ducts collapsed, a mass of dystrophic calcifications pulling the nipple inwards — where it remains.

Breasts and mothering.

Bodies hold so much love as we face mortality. Bones break, breasts grow tumours, eyes cloud, but love...

I had moved to another country thinking I would slow down, shift direction, but the pandemic still had me scurrying to save Cinnamon Press. Work piled up... late nights, 2.00 a.m. held by a screen, doing *just* one more thing...

By mid 2024 the exhaustion was unmanageable. After twenty-four years of managing the conditions left behind by assaults, I *know* I must shepherd energy, follow the rhythms of my body, but instead I pushed on, even during the sabbatical from work for Cinnamon Press. The year had been littered with symptoms and tests — the rib that seemed to break for no reason, digestive issues, rashes I'd never previously experienced, dry eyes and throat...

During September in the UK an otherwise enchanted month had been punctuated by mouth ulcers and skin rashes, painfully dry eyes, joint aches, a swinging temperature, fevers coming and going. All year my thick hair had been thinning. Being deaf in my left ear since childhood, I've always had poor balance, but the dizziness had heightened. And the swollen ankle, its veins like bruises, throbbed the length of my calf.

Through the year a range of conditions had been suggested, tried on... Nothing fitted.

A month into the sabbatical, I began to notice that when I was deep in flow, writing, my temperature would rise and a butterfly rash appeared on my face. The jigsaw pieces finally settled — systemic lupus erythematosus.

It seemed an odd diagnosis at sixty-three, but had likely gone undiagnosed for years. Perhaps the first flares came in the early years of sickness, fatigue, and inflammation after the assaults. Perhaps two bouts of Covid had contributed to it flaring again. Or maybe my body was simply insisting there must be loss, a letting go like the forest in winter, before a new story.

Ageing and permeable to the ancestor I will become, loving a life that death will touch, reminded me of a day during my first herbal apprenticeship. Each of us introduced a tree and its properties, the final tree, at dusk on a November evening, was yew. A young woman invited us to take a berry and eat the flesh without swallowing, or in any way biting into, the seed at the centre of the aril.

The berry — small, fleshy, magenta — contains a single deadly seed. Even swallowing it whole and allowing it to pass through the body might be fatal or make a person extremely sick. Every part of yew is poisonous. Every part except the pink juicy flesh of the aril, a tiny sweet peach around its toxic heart.

The ground around yew is brown, no grass grows. The gnarled trunk can be enormous, as though several ancient and crooked trunks have merged. Often the trunk will divide and arch into the ground. There are yews known to be a thousand, two thousand years old, one, in the churchyard of St. Digain's in Llangernyw, Wales, is between four and five thousand years old. Its ancient bark is furrowed and ridged, scaly and flaking. Its core has been lost, but the enormous offshoots stand with a girth of almost eleven metres.

With the invitation to eat the aril without swallowing the seed, came the question: Who is the ancestor you want to become?

I took a berry, ate the flesh, held the tiny seed in my hand, the beginning of a tree that could live for thousands of years.

Sacred to the Druids, yew is a tree of cycles and regeneration. Its bark is brittle, but its heartwood as flexible as it is hard. Yew stands on the threshold between life and death, watches over graveyards, guards those we mourn. The toxins of its bark are used in chemotherapy and its longevity and ability to plant parts of its trunk to become new trees, bear witness to resilience. How one life flows into the next and the next. And though every part of yew is poisonous, a host of fungi, birds and insects thrive in its ecosystem.

Death and resurrection.

Yew takes the long view.

Clairvoyance — the word that means 'clear sight'.

Who is the ancestor you want to become?

Moving to the forest, on the threshold of elderhood, at the heart's farthest edge, I have been asking that question since that day.

Each of us will become an ancestor, but for now we love what death can touch.

Into the liminal

In the deep winter of 2024, I taught a course on herbs of the fifth season, a space between the cycles of the year.

The world was darkening, yet the forest was bright. Early November — days of pale clear sky, that reminded me of Casilda, who wore only white and the palest blue, the bleached blue that haloes the sun. Oaks in flashes of carnelian, sepia paper, brittling to the ground, birches fluttering ripe gamboge and amber, striating the light, beeches clinging to leaves — raw sienna and auburn, a single lemon flame of larch, while hawthorn flaunted leaves of many colours — carmine edged in lime, golden syrup, cinnamon-mottled, and elders tendered coral, vermillion, rust…

How do we face what is coming? How do we make art when the fragile, breath-taking beauty of this world is under siege — when waters are poisoned or stolen, species disappear, children die alone under the rubble of their bombed homes, places of safety become tombs, forests burn, women's bodily autonomy and reproductive rights are threatened, land turns to desert, a population is starved to death, trans folks' human rights are dismantled, coasts flood, young men in despair take their own lives, refugees are refused safe haven, genocide is redefined as self-defence?

Yet still the forest put on its beauty in the face of winter's cyclic death. Still whales lullabied oceans. Still owls serenaded the moon.

We can't know what new story lies on the other side of any moment, only that there will be one.

> And we are here as on a darkling plain

Matthew Arnold writes in 'On Dover Beach'.

And on that dark plain — still we can love.

There is a story from Welsh mythology of a girl made from flowers by Math and Gwydion to be a wife for Lleu, who is born after rape and cursed by his mother never to marry a human wife. With Blodeuwedd as his wife, Lleu is able to rule the land, for she is the Empress of the Tarot, the sovereignty of the land, the world in bloom.

But who can take the earth against her will?

Blodeuwedd falls in love with Gronw, but Lleu will never release her and so the couple plot to kill Lleu and free Blodeuwedd. The problem is that Lleu cannot be killed, either outdoors or in, not on horse nor on foot, and only with a spearhead cast during a sacred period of time. So Gronw spends a year and a day making a spearhead — the period of sacred time — while Blodeuwedd persuades Lleu to demonstrate how difficult it would be to kill him.

Lleu prepares a bath at the side of the river, has a thatched roof erected over it and stands in the bathwater — neither inside nor out… He clambers onto the edge of the bath, reaches one foot out and rests it on the back of a goat. Neither on horse nor on foot, he tells Blodeuwedd and, as he is speaking, Gronw's arrow flies towards him and lodges in his side. Dead. But is he? The slumped body rises, an injured eagle, bleeding, but able to take flight. Math (Lleu's father) and Gwydion (Math's uncle) search for Lleu and treat his wounds, bring him back to his human form. And then they search for the lovers and when they find them Gronw is killed, but Blodeuwedd they transform into an owl, a bird of night and death.

And still to this day in the land where Blodeuwedd was made, her name means both flower-face and owl. She wanted to be flowers, but not owned. She wanted to be flowers — oak and nettle, primrose, bean, broom, meadowsweet, burdock, chestnut and hawthorn — but they made her an owl.

In my writing room, the picture of Blodeuwedd by the artist Pat Gregory (an image done for a poetry collection, *skindancing* by Susan

Richardson), shows Blodeuwedd as a young woman in a red dress, gazing into a mirror. An owl, its talons and eyes petals amongst its feathers, gazes back. And under the image is the legend, 'I'm still here'.

She wants to be flowers, as do I — in my writing, my encounters with the world, human and more-than-human — tender, open… And yet she chose love, freedom, risk, her own joy… allowed the possibility of death or transformation for the sake of a different story.

But this choice — flowers or owl — is a false dichotomy. The owl too tenders the world, mothers and sings, lullabies her chicks, soft feathers a nest, yet knows she will need her talons, her wings.

Not all darkness overwhelms or scares us. The safe cave with its fire that protects, invites stories to be shared, flickers light into the dark, the rich dark earth brimming with fertility, the winter months that invite us to rest and restore… It is not light *or* dark, flowers *or* owl, personal survival *or* the survival of others far away, self-compassion *or* radical generosity…

In the forest the colours are entrancing. An Otherworld in this liminal season of elder.

The elder tree by our gate was wounded not long after we moved to the forest, but she healed, and soon after we noticed a scatter of tiny new elders. One, outside my writing room window, fills with berries in autumn. Elder to accompany us through the winter.

I'd imagined the sabbatical would give me so much space, but I had not reckoned with illness, how hungry my body was for rest… the days contracting.

I sat with elder, a tree who straddles worlds, growing along boundaries, along the edge of water, between wild and cultivated lands. Elder branches were left on graves — a sign that the deceased was at peace if they blossomed in spring.

She is beautiful in summer, frothy and cheerful, but it is from

Samhain through Winter Solstice to Imbolc that I feel her power. A tree of ambiguities. I sat with her at the cusp of New Year in 2021, a year of lockdowns, our first in France, a year of bereavement... And I sat with her for hours during the winter of 2024.

Elder's leaves and berries are poisonous when raw, but transform into rich nourishment when heated. In folk traditions it was disastrous to burn elder, yet the root of her name in Anglo-Saxon means 'to kindle' and her hollow stems can be used to blow air into fire to make it blaze. She has been feared, yet is often a graveyard tree, protecting the dead.

Associated with ancestors, protection and faery magic, elder has strong boundaries. The music made through elder stems could warn of death, yet she is also a herb of life.

Elder, like yew, is connected with clear sight. The tea from her flowers is a tonic for the eyes, a giver of vision.

Sitting in elder's shade, breathing in winter air, scents of damp and woodsmoke, the sky ice-white behind banks of coal-grey cloud, I listen…

There's a practice in herbalism — 'heart resonance' or 'heart coherence' — of attending to plants with the heart. More and more we understand that our hearts, physically as well as emotionally, synchronise with those we love — it happens in couples, between mothers and infants, with close friends, in safe social groups. It isn't limited to the human world.

The heart is an organ of perception. Its electromagnetic field can be detected several feet away, 65% of its cells are made of neurones, over 40,000 of them, sending signals to the brain. Memory and emotions are held there. The ways in which we construct the world.

When we enter a state of heart coherence our nervous system fills with dopamine, cortisol drops and there is a rise in a natural steroid that helps with heart-health and depression, DHEA. When lovers whose hearts are in resonance touch, pain levels fall. The heart is the secret fire of alchemists, a means of connection.

Sitting with elder, my body relaxes, gaze becomes diffuse, breath gentles, everything softening, opening, allowing my heart to expand, settle, become permeable, tender, allowing me to attend.

Slowly, so slowly, my heart unfolds and elder speaks — in images and sensations, memories like fragments of film, scent, the air on my skin, the voice of a harp — *Sambucus*. There is no time, no words. Only as I rouse to consciousness do words form.

What are you doing here?

Epilogue

I followed a fork in the path to the forest, a place to remain open and permeable.

What are you doing here?

What story do you want to live?

At the heart's farthest edge nothing is fixed. I find myself living with unknowing, constantly recalibrating the daily rhythms of what it might mean to craft a creative life in a perilous world.

I'm here because of a chain of decisions and events over decades that could have gone in so many other directions. Whatever forks in the path we choose, we all know where the path ends, but we are story-making creatures fascinated by where we came from and the stories along the way. My stories are spun from fallible memories, selected and polished across decades. I've carried them to Finistère, to a quirky house with a garden that floods, renovations that seem endless, mice, bats and ants who want to live indoors…

The story that L saw in me at the age of eleven, of the four-year-old alone in a busy town who found trance in a stained glass window. The story of a child who found another world in a stream where sticklebacks swam, a stone's throw from eighty-square miles of heavily-polluting chemical and steel works. Of mothering four home-educated children and of a faith that made history before becoming amnesia. Stories of grief for parents, a lost sister, a broken marriage, an assaulted body. The story of finding A.

The night before my herbal exam, I fall asleep to the song of owls. In

Breton lore, the owl is the white lady, the bird of Ankou, servant of death who gathers souls. Death and rebirth. Flowers and owls. 'Finistère' means 'the end of the land/world' and also 'the head (or start) of the world', 'Penn-ar-Bed' in Breton. Most endings are also beginnings.

At the end of the world, I become a herbalist.

Three months later, at the end of March, 2025, I travel to the coast with A., to a place where the headland is surrounded by sea and the wind keens always. Behind a hunched bank, its back to the ocean, a swathe of wood violets, gorse — abundant and golden — speckled with sea campion, white stars against green grasses, blackthorn — fierce and exquisite — peoples the heath, guards the stony paths, and the sea, turquoise and teal, scintillates to sun's pulse and moon's pull, breaks in foam and spume — liquid towers white against ochre granite. Early April, the sky a wash of blues — hot cyan to linen smoke, the bay in the distance a dust-blue shadow. Further out, on this needle of land, ocean swells to the thrill of wind around a crest of gale-sculpted rocks, and a water pipit hymns the day with a fast fall of sweetness, insistent as summer cicadas.

Forest and coast, a spit of Celtic earth that sings of a home I might never have known.

The last three months have vanished in work. I've been busy since I was three years old. But for just as long, I've also known how to disappear into trance and here, lulled by the sea, I sleep deeply and well, walk along the beach and out to the headland, delighting in flowers singing spring awake —

sea pink thrift

fat daisies

primrose

valerian

rosemary, fragrant and purple

blackthorn

sea campion

dandelion

violet

pink sorrel

gorse

three-cornered leek

lesser celandine

greater periwinkle

common bluebell

scurvy-grass

marsh stitchwort

— and in the cottage garden, a single calla lily.

What are you doing here?

I'm doing what we all do — exploring ways to live a small life well in an aching world. I have gathered love letters from a puddle of colour reflected on the stone floor in a church in Teesside, a friend who gave me another name, a lover who is steadfast oak to my airy-mistletoe-mind, a house nestled in Welsh slate and a dwelling in a forest in Finistère, where plants and trees whisper. Together they weave a story along the heart's farthest edge.

Shall we see where the story might lead?

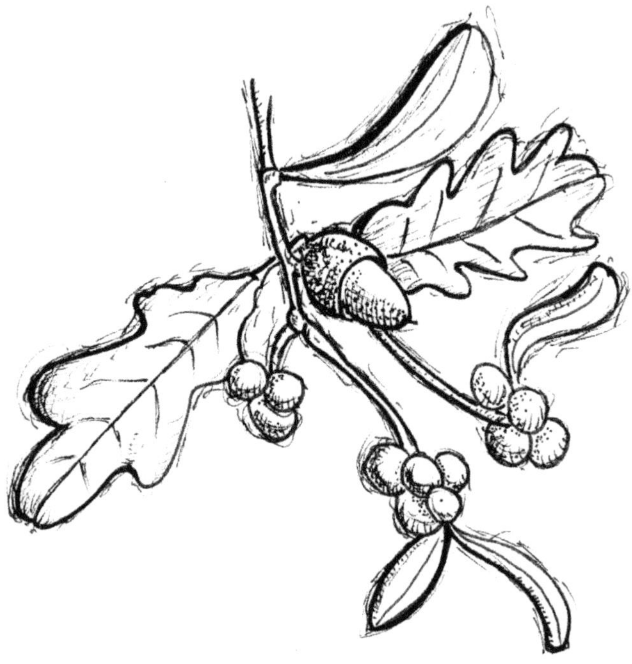

Notes and Acknowledgements

A note on pronouns

The plant world is not a world of false dichotomies and simplistic binaries. We experience plants through the lens of our particular beings. I find myself relating to many plants and trees as 'she', some as 'he' and others as 'they'. There is nothing definitive in this. Your experience will be just that — *yours* — and the pronouns you use for the more-than-human world will reflect as much about you as about that world. It was ever thus and no one can define your particular experience for you.

References

p.13 & p.96 'It's the time you have wasted for your rose that makes your rose so important … You become responsible forever for what you've tamed.' & p.96: 'It is only with the heart that one can see rightly; what is essential is invisible to the eye.' From *The Little Prince,* Antoine de Saint-Exupéry, trans. Katherine Woods, 1943.

p.22: *If a lion could speak, we wouldn't understand him* is a paraphrase of Wittgenstein in *Philosophische Untersuchungen*, later translated as *Philosophical Investigations.*

p.30: 'somewhere a horse chestnut has just been struck by lightning, and half of it split away.'— from a scene in *Jane Eyre.* After Rochester kisses Jane for the first time, the next morning Adele comes to tell her about the tree.

p.39 & 90: 'I will work harder' is spoken by Boxer in *Animal Farm,* George Orwell, 1945.

p.74: 'To lose one parent, Mr. Worthing, may be regarded as a misfortune; to lose both looks like carelessness.' from *The Importance of Being Earnest,* Oscar Wilde, first performed 1895, published 1899.

p.90: 'Style is a very simple matter…' Virginia Woolf, *The Letters of Virginia Woolf: vol III, 1923-1928*, ed. Nigel Nicolson & Joanne Trautman.

p.96: 'Sing a song of May-time' is a slight mis-remembering of the hymn by Frederick A. Jackson, first published in *Sunday School Hymnary,* 1905.

p.97: 'seeing with the unworn sides of the eyes' *The Journals of Henry David Thoreau*, 1837-1861.

p.171: 'And we are here as on a darkling plain', Matthew Arnold 'On Dover Beach' from *New Poems*, 1867.

p.174: There is a growing body of research on heart resonance, including as a pain-relief:
https://www.sciencedaily.com/releases/2017/06/170621125313.htm

Prose poems from *Stale Bread & Miracles,* Cinnamon Press. 2009, 2017.

'Return to Tŷ Meirion' from *Slate Voices*, Jan Fortune & Mavis Gulliver, Cinnamon Press, 2014.

Haiku and Celtic seasonal poems from *at world's end, begin*, Jan Fortune, Cinnamon Press, 2023.

A fictionalised version of Casilda's story can be found in *Casilda of the Rising Moon*, Elizabeth Borton de Treviño, 1967, New York: Farrar, Straus and Giroux and also in the final book of the Casilda Trilogy: *This is the End of the Story; A Remedy for All Things* and *For Hope is Always Born*, Jan Fortune, Cinnamon Press.

Acknowledgements

I am grateful to Adam Craig for listening to the chapters of this book (often several times), for his reading and comments and for his beautiful artwork. To Kerri ní Dochartaigh for her careful reading and generous feedback on the manuscript and for her kind words for the cover. To John Barnie for meticulous copy-editing and for his thoughtful cover quote. And to Marya Hornbacher for graciously reading the book and providing not only cover copy, but friendship.

Huge thanks to all those who supported the production of this book: Sumaya Abuhaidar, Bruce Ackerley, Maria Americo, Deb Baker, Carolyn Cahalane, Bobbie Darbyshire, Tricia Durdey, Anne Dunford, Ellis Elliott, Judith Field, Yvonne Govan, Michela Griffith, Angharad Griffiths, Rosemary Hector, Karen Howard, Tracey Iceton, Nick Jones, Sue Lewis, Dana Littlepage Smith, Isabelle Llasera, Susie Mawhinney, Denise O'Connor, Fiona Owen, Liliana Pasterska, Tom Proverbs-Garbett, Rachel Retallick, Kay Syrad, Jill Teague, Bonnie Thurston, George Walker, Roger White, Clare Whittaker, Helen May Williams, Rachel Wolfreys, Patricia Helen Wooldridge, Jeremy Worman, Kathy Wrightson.

Along the path, there have been encounters with places, people, creatures and plants that have made all the difference. Thank you. Amongst the humans who have walked parts of this path with me, I'm especially grateful to my paternal grandparents, Chris & Annie, and to Dennie, Ann (née Fortune), Lorna, Ian, John Smith, Dick & Yvonne, Kirsty, Elaine, Steve & Sheila, John Sweet, Rowan W, Michael H, Michael S, Charmion, Bernice, Lizzie, Sally, Anne, April, Jonathan, Peter M, Peter P, Neill, Angela, Karen & Narnik, Nicholas, Paul, Janet, Tom & Sherry, Gladys & Les, Veronica & Charlie, Dr Manyweathers, Bobbie, Kate & George, Sarah & Dafydd, Michelle, John B, Isabelle, Héloïse & Cédric, Caroline, Kerri and Marya.

And above all, deep thanks to my family — Rowan-Echo, Tamsyn, Cottia, Seth, Finn, Merlin and Iris, and to Adam, always.

www.ingramcontent.com/pod-product-compliance
Ingram Content Group UK Ltd.
Pitfield, Milton Keynes, MK11 3LW, UK
UKHW041839310326
469526UK00011B/39/J

9 781788 641937